Robert Collyer

Nature and Life

Sermons

Robert Collyer

Nature and Life
Sermons

ISBN/EAN: 9783337114091

Printed in Europe, USA, Canada, Australia, Japan

Cover: Foto ©Lupo / pixelio.de

More available books at **www.hansebooks.com**

NATURE AND LIFE:

SERMONS

BY

ROBERT COLLYER,

PASTOR OF UNITY CHURCH, CHICAGO.

FOURTH EDITION.

BOSTON:
HORACE B. FULLER,
SUCCESSOR TO WALKER, FULLER, & CO., 245, WASHINGTON STREET
CHICAGO: JOHN R. WALSH.
1867.

Entered, according to Act of Congress, in the year 1867, by

HORACE B. FULLER,

In the Clerk's Office of the District Court of the District of Massachusetts

CAMBRIDGE:
STEREOTYPED AND PRINTED BY
JOHN WILSON AND SON.

TO

NAHOR AUGUSTUS STAPLES,

NOW IN HEAVEN,

This Book

IS DEDICATED AS A TOKEN OF

UNDYING LOVE.

PREFACE.

I LET this little book go out into the world, feeling almost as if it were one of my children. I cannot be indifferent to its reception, because I love it. So I trust it will be welcome wherever it goes, — that friends will be glad to see it for my sake, and strangers for its own. If it should be blessed with a long life, I shall rejoice greatly; but, if it die early, I shall still be glad it was born.

R. C.

MAY 20, 1867.

CONTENTS.

		PAGE
I.	Root and Flower	1
II.	What a Leaf Said	23
III.	The Treasures of the Snow	43
IV.	Light on a Hidden Way	61
V.	The Folly of Solomon	83
VI.	Faith	102
VII.	Hope	119
VIII.	Love	139
IX.	Ascending and Descending Angels	161
X.	The Fear of God	178
XI.	A Talk to Mothers	198
XII.	Healing and Hurting Shadows	216
XIII.	The Hither Side	236
XIV.	The Book of Psalms	256
XV.	The Battle-field of Fort Donelson	274
XVI.	Omega	296

SERMONS.

I.

ROOT AND FLOWER.

JOHN xii. 20–25: "And there were certain Greeks among them that came up to worship at the feast. The same came therefore to Philip, which was of Bethsaida of Galilee, and desired him, saying, Sir, we would see Jesus. Philip cometh and telleth Andrew: and again, Andrew and Philip tell Jesus. And Jesus answered them, saying, The hour is come that the Son of man should be glorified. Verily, verily, I say unto you, Except a corn of wheat fall into the ground and die, it abideth alone: but, if it die, it bringeth forth much fruit. He that loveth his life shall lose it, and he that hateth his life in this world shall keep it unto life eternal."

I WENT once, in the last days of June, to see an old friend in the country, who has consecrated his life to trees and flowers. When I came away, he gave me something wrapped in a piece of paper, bidding me select the best spot in my garden, when I got home, and plant it. "For," he added, "that is a very choice flower, sir,—one of the most beautiful things you ever saw in your life." I left my friend, and started home; and, when I had got well out of his sight, of course I undid the paper, that I might look at my treasure. It was as queer, unpromising a thing to look at, as I ever saw. At the first glance, you would take it for a poor, haggard old onion. There was not a speck of beauty about it, that I should desire it. Then I put my flower back into the paper, brought it home, and planted it just as I was directed; and when I had done this, I began to ponder and wonder over this great mystery of planting and growing and flowering. I said to myself,—"What are my conceptions of what is to come out of my dark, forbidding bulb? I never saw the flower, I suppose, in my life. I have no certain idea what it is like. It may resemble a sunflower or a peony or a daisy or a bluebell. If I carry a single tooth pried out of the limestone to Professor Owen, he will sketch me an outline of the animal that used it, though this be the first fragment ever seen of a thing that died out ten thousand years before the first man. But I may carry a fragment of this root to the Owen of plants, if there be one, and ask him to search in it for the flower; and I suppose he must fail to tell me what it will be, because there seems to be no possible link between the bare grain and the body as it pleases God. And then this choicest spot in the garden, — what did my friend mean by that?. If I understand him, he meant a place of the strongest possible contrasts, — a place bare to the sun and the night and the wind and the rain; where I had gathered the heaviest proportion of shard, refuse, and decay; a place where life has to do battle with darkness and death, and to draw from them its richest elements of beauty and perfume. And then what have I done? My friend gave me this flower, as he called it, folded carefully as if it were a jewel of price; and, carefully as he gave it, I brought it home. But, when I got home, I put it down into this grim earth, this fragment of the measureless waste of land, and left it there. Had I not better keep it in some safe casket, or fold it to my heart, until I see the beauty that my friend has promised? Is it possible, — is it ind.spensable in that will of God which I have been taught to call the order of nature, that the only way to come at the beauty and glory is that it shall be put away and buried out of my sight?

Can it be true, that the way to find what I want is to lose it; that the transcendent form and color and perfume of August must depend upon the decay of June?"

Well, friends, these are some of the hinted questionings that whispered themselves out of my poor dry root, and I could give them but one answer; namely, "These seeming contradictions are only so because I do not know enough. And I can only know as I walk by faith; for faith, above all things, makes the discords of the present the harmonies of the future."

It is one of the many curious things that look out at us from almost every page of the Gospels, to assure us that the Gospels themselves are substantially fragments out of the real life and times of Jesus Christ, — that these men, who had come to the feast at Jerusalem and requested to see Jesus, should be Greeks, at that time probably the most inquisitive and newsy race on the earth. They had come, I presume, from Corinth or Ephesus; and, when they went back home, the first question would be, "What's the news?" Now, the news was Jesus; his name and fame had gone out into all Jewry. He was just then the common subject of discussion in the city gates and synagogues; and it would be a great thing for them, when they got back home, to say, "We have seen Jesus, and talked with him." And the answer of Christ to their request, though it seems at the first glance to be no answer at all, touches the very heart of all such question and answer, and is, beside that, a beautiful instance of the rich, transcendental nature of this Son of God: "Except a corn of wheat fall into the ground and die, it abideth alone; but, if it die, it bringeth forth much fruit." As if he would say, "These men want to see me. What can they gain by that? There is nothing to see in me. If they want to see me, they must wait until I go away, and the world sees me no more. What they will see is not me. The root is not the flower. This common, foot-sore man, with this poor, brown face, so thin and worn that men think I may be nearly fifty, while I am still but thirty, — what can I be to men whose ideal is Apollo? I cannot sing with Homer; I cannot speculate with Plato; I cannot unloose the seals with Euclid, or bear men on the mighty tides of eloquence with Demosthenes. Phidias made the marble speak;

Apelles made the canvas glow; I made ploughs and carts and ox-yokes and stools. They cannot see me. My simple words about God and man, and duty and destiny, would be foolishness to them. Let them wait until the world burns with the lustre of what is sprung out of me. When I have risen and stand with the martyr in the fire; when I shine in the catacombs until there is no need of the sun; when I have whispered my comfort and confidence to millions of desolate souls, who are now, and will be looking at what seems to them the fearful vacancy of the hereafter; when I have created new homes for purity and peace to dwell in, and brought men and women and children back to the Divine will; when the love and truth and self-sacrifice of which God has made me, though I seem but a poor peasant, shall have done what all the genius of all the ages has failed to do; when I have hushed the fevered heart of the world to rest, and quickened it into a new life, — then they can see me. But I must die to live. The burial comes, then the resurrection. I must be absent as a root, or I can never be present as a flower."

Such, as I understand it, is the meaning folded,

not only in my text, but also in the richest life of the world. Just as this most celestial soul was folded in a life about which there is a very early application of those old prophecies of some chosen one who should be as a root out of a dry ground, whose face should be marred more than that of any man, who should have no form nor comeliness in him, so that, when men saw him, there should be no beauty that they should desire him; and as God cast him, so folded, into the place which, of all others at that time, held the heaviest proportion of shard and refuse hastening to decay, — cast him into that place as the choicest spot in the garden of the world, and then, by sunlight and darkness and dryness and rain and life and death, wrought out his purpose, until the flower came up, in the full time, to fill the world with wonder and blessing, — so it will be with God's best blossom and fruit for ever and ever.

The world bends with infinite tenderness over the story of that woman who had no beauty and no blessing, out on the Yorkshire moors. We pity her for the dismal, scranny school of her childhood, where food for the outer and the inner life was alike hard and crusty and mouldy. We pity her for the lonely drudgery, so hapless and so hopeless, out in Brussels, as we see her sit down to it, while her wings bleed beating the bars of her cage, and the music soars within her, —

> "And the life still drags her downward
> To its level, day by day, —
> What is fine within her growing
> Coarse to sympathetic clay."

Our lips tremble as we see that striving after some touch of grace and beauty to deck the hard, gray home, though it embody itself in no better thing than a bright little frock and a pair of tiny red shoes; yet to see the poor blossom of grace and beauty shrivelling in the fire, put there and held there by a father harder than the home. We watch her, a woman while yet a child, — a woman, because other little children, still more helpless, are motherless, and can find no other nature large enough to take them in and understand and adopt them; a sister in all sweet, ingenuous, simple ways; a mother in all wise, overbending care and love; and then, at last, a woman grown, walking over great stretches of wild country, that she might be alone with that other Father and Mother, the Father and Mother of us all, and gather strength and courage from the communion, to go back and bear her burden of a stern, half-mad father, and a reckless, lost brother, and a bare, rugged life; then we say, " Oh! why was not such a soul clothed in the beauty of Juno, and born in the vale of Tempe, in the golden days, the first-born and nursling of a queen?" But we say this no longer when the flower unfolds to the sun, — when her books and her life, in all their variant strength and fulness, reveal the mystery of the homely enfolding, the rank, sharp contrasts of the garden-plat and the hot days and dark nights; for we see in the flower brimming with refreshment and blessing to thousands, how not to the beauty of the goddess, not to the flowery meadows and bosky dells of Arcadia, not to the firstborn and nursling of a queen, could this power come; but to such a soul, set in such a place, to battle through and gather all the influences of such a life.

And so, again, dear, quaint, loving Charles Lamb flowered out of the sharp contrasts of Fleet Street and the South-sea House, and that other influence and element of bitterness almost too terrible to mention. No man who has been touched by the sweet beauty and merry twinkling humor of Elia and the Letters, can realize readily how it is that this airy, sprightly, and most wise, genial soul, could ever gather such nurture in the shadows of Christ's Hospital, and the eternal dust and din of London. One imagines that the endless drudgery of the desk, and the shadow of a home where no face of wife or child ever lighted at the sound of his footstep, ought to have withered him up; and so it ought, but for one thing that flashes down into the mystery, and, besides the fact of his endowment, solves the problem. When Charles Lamb was a young man, standing at the portals of life, with that rich nature beating in his heart, his sister Mary, in a sudden passion of insanity, did the most awful deed that daughter can do to mother. Then, when the dust was given to the dust, this young man said, "If I remain as I am, and make my sister a home, there may be months or years at a time when she can live with me in freedom and comfort; but, if I put her away, there can be no future for her but the asylum all the days of her life." Then the young man buried his rich nature in the soil of that home. And, in all his life, he never told the world what he had done; revealing himself so frankly in all beside, there is no hint of that prime revelation which might open all the rest. He buried his life. And, were we ignorant of this great law of what is rich soil to a noble root, we would say, Now he will wither away and die. But, lo! God brings out of that burial a flower, whose perfume and beauty charm the world. Had he saved his life, it may be he had lost it; but, because he gave it, he saved it; because he went into the darkness, he sprang into the light; he rose because he was buried, and his uttermost loss became his most transcendent gain.

There is nothing more touching to me in all literature, than those poems and letters of Burns that reveal to us this great fact of adverse influences perfecting the Divine purpose. We hear eminent critics deplore the fact that Burns wasted his powers. They say he ought to have written an epic. Friends, Burns did write an epic; and the subject was the battle of a soul with its physical, social, and spiritual adversaries, — an epic perhaps the most significant that ever was written. And his whole life, and every line in his poems, blend together to make it; and it trembles all over with this truth of a life found in the losing, and lost in the finding. Born in the worst period and place of a fossilized Calvinism, he drew from that very fossil the richest nurture for a broad and catholic trust in the Infinite Love. Placed where a free expression of opinion in religious speculation was counted atheism, and in politics treason, the very bonds that were laid on his soul to keep him down, quickened him into some of the deepest and grandest utterances for freedom that ever rang through the world. Taught from his cradle that our human nature is utterly abhorrent and bad, the angels trust not each other with a more perfect trust than that which filled his soul toward humanity. Loving as few men ever loved, fewer ever told, as he did, what love can do to lift a man near to heaven, or to sink him into a great deep. No man ever painted such an interior as the "Cotter's Saturday Night," or by implication called such solemn penalties upon his own soul for causing the mother to weep, and the father to hang his head in such a place. And out of that bitter time and place, with that passionate, sinful, sorrowful nature, the result of the life, in the whole breadth of it, remains one of the richest flowers that ever blossomed on the world. A Scottish peasant, deplorably poor, he left the world richer beyond all price. Born into the lap of a grim and forbidding time, the time was glorified in his birth. More selfish than most sinners, he was more unselfish than almost any saint. And well he might have cried out, " Let no man look at me who wants to see me, or try to find the result of my life by the measure of what he sees. I shall die, broken down by poverty and sorrow and sin; but I shall rise again, and lead captivity captive, and receive gifts for men. Old sectarian antagonisms will forget to be hard and unmerciful, as they hear me pleading; and the fires of a nobler political faith glow for ever in the words I have uttered of the rights of man. Men shall look more frankly into each other's faces, when they hear me cry, ' A man's a man for a' that;' and the atheist gulp down his sneer, as he ponders over my rebuke. My better nature shall make good men better; my wild cries for pardon teach the sinner afresh the curse of sin. My life was lost, that it might be found; I died that I might bear much fruit."

Now, I have mentioned these representative lives, bearing on different sides of the thought before us, in order that you may see, by these examples, how I want to urge upon you the fact, that this clear and steady insight into the correspondence between nature in the plant and nature in the man, which comes out so constantly in the teachings of Christ, is weighted with a deep meaning, and is for ever open to suggest rich lessons for the soul.

And this first of all, — that this present, personal-bounded life is but faintly understood, it is so poor in comparison with what shall come out of it, if we are steady to its great central purpose.

My shrivelled bulb, darkling there under the soil; this homely, near-sighted woman, sneering at the "Methodies;" this poor, stuttering London clerk, watching his sometimes insane sister; this Ayrshire peasant, whose highest preferment was to be a gauger, and whose heart exulted because he had "dinnered wi' a lord," — a lord whose only hope of being remembered now on this earth lies in that single dinner; this peasant man of Galilee, whose brothers did not believe in him, — all these instances strike the truth home, that we see but a poor hint now of the glory resting on our life, to be discovered when that life shall be made perfect.

That man walking over the hills of Jewry in the old time was no more like our worshipful Christ and Son of God, if you had seen him, than the May root is like the August flower. That quiet woman, before she wrote "Jane Eyre," was no more to the world than the woman hidden to-day in our prairies or backwoods, who shall yet reveal herself and be central to the world. Charles Lamb and Robert Burns, could they come back, would find nations waiting to do them homage, on the very spot where they felt most deeply the bitterness of neglect. And this, not so much because the world was blind to their beauty, as that this beauty had not yet flowered out. They died, " not having received the promise, but seeing it afar off; God having reserved some better thing for us, that they without us should not be made perfect."

Then there is this lesson, that those very elements of decay and death we fear will hinder, to the true soul will not hinder, but help; nay, be vital and essential to the great purpose for which that soul came, and to which it tends.

I know of nothing more fatal, in all outward seeming, than Jewry to Christ, and Ayrshire to Burns, and Fleet Street to Lamb, and Haworth to Charlotte Brontë. If God, in every one of these instances, had revealed to me the conditional as the root of the resulting life, I think I should have besought him every time to alter the decision, and not plant such holy and noble natures in such a dismal soil; while the place I should have chosen, had it been left to me, would probably be as if I had kept the root my friend gave me safely locked in my desk,— never thinking how it is out of the very contest with these antagonisms, that the choicest power and grace must spring: as the farce of saying mass by the scented priests in Rome made Luther say it with a deeper reverence, and more anxious searching for its grace. But, above all, may we not see this greatest lesson, that more profit comes to the soul, and all related to it, out of separation and darkness and death, in God's good time, than can ever come out of union and light and life? "Except a corn of wheat fall into the ground and die, it abideth alone; but, if it die, it will bring forth much fruit."

I suppose no men that ever lived would be more ready than these apostles to say, "We grant this, if you mean a grain of wheat; but we cannot see it, if you mean the life of a man." Yet they themselves were to furnish one of the most striking applications of the fact ever found in human history. While the Messiah was with them, they blundered over his sayings, hesitated whether they could go with him, held a divided love, and saw through a glass darkly, as I saw the August flower in the root of June. But when he died and was gone, then he came back to them in all his glory and power. When they had lost him, and darkness and death had taken him seemingly into their heart, then came the resurrection. Every word he had said became radiant with tenderness and truth and love. His deeds caught a new meaning. His life filled before them into an ever-growing wonder; and he was transfigured for ever, not to three men, but to the universe. Then, as the great memories filled them, their sense grew ever clearer of what their Friend had been; but even that, at last, was lost in the sense of what he was. So they loved him, and labored and lived and died for him; and, when their time came, went singing, with a most glorious and transcendent exultation, into the shadow of death, because his light, shining through the shadow, goldened all the way.

Now, this is where the truth under discussion comes most urgently home to every one of us. The time comes again and again, when we must bury the best we have, and leave it in the soil,— sever some precious belonging of life for duty with Lamb; or find sin or circumstance, sever it with Burns. The prime condition of a life ever found, is a life ever lost. But there are times when we all feel poor and bare and sad for our losses, and wonder whether it was not all wrong when the treasure was taken away. I tell you, if we are poor because we stand true to life and duty, we are poor only as the sower is poor, because he has to cast his wheat into the furrow, and then wait for the sheaves of harvest, — poor as I was poor, because my flower-root was not treasured where it would remain as it was, but was cast where a life was waiting to receive and re-create it, as true in its way and mighty as the life of the first archangel.

Our poverty, then, is our wealth, and our loss our gain. If our life is as God will, yet is bare, it is only as the granary is bare in June. That very bareness is the prophecy of plenty; and fulness alone in June might bring grave reason to fear, that there might be sparseness and hunger in January. When I sow my good treasure broadcast, as Christ did; when I give myself with what I am giving, — then, as the earth never fails of her harvest, but, in the Old World or the New, will surely bring us our daily bread, so the soul can never fail of her divine returns. Here or yonder, in the full time, comes the full blessing; the flower flashing out glory, the fields laughing with plenty.♦

> "Then who can murmur and misdoubt,
> When God's great bounty finds him out?"

And just as I can gather and deepen this faith; as I can realize, though I have never seen, the beauty of my August,—I shall be ready to plant my root, to let my wheat fall into the ground and die, to give my life. Our great temptation is to hold on to the seed-corn. We are in agony because of the sowing. When the angel comes and takes our treasure, we say we will go too, that we may die also. But the hand so masterful and yet so gentle takes our treasure, and casts it into its grave; and then the hope and love and life of our life is dead.

Dead, did I say? What means this story of the summer? Is not every day proclaiming through all the land, that what was seeming death is unconquerable life? Death has no dominion; death is lost in victory. The resurrection comes while I am going to look at the grave, and weep there, and count my losses and recount my poverty. And then the shining ones tell me the great secret, and send me on my way, lost in wonder and solemn joy.

So it has been with our nation. Our root was buried in the rank soil of decay and death; and many cried out that the noble thing perfected out of a former summer, and watered by the tears and enriched with the blood of the fathers, was clean lost. It was because God had taken it out of its dead coverings, and cast it into the heart of elements that throb with life, as the earth throbs with the summer sun. It was buried that it might rise. The flowering of the former summer was over and done; the blossoms of our national holiness had withered away; the root alone was left. We held on to that through the winter, thank God; but then we wanted to hold on to it through the summer also: we feared to trust it to the new spring. The root, withered as it was, was what we wanted. But our Father is the husbandman; and he buried the root out of our sight. It was because there was as sure a hope for the nation as there is for June roses. We had to watch painfully for it, — to wrestle with awful oppositions through a dark night. But so does the farmer watch and wrestle for his harvest. Canker-worm and caterpillar take their toll; wind and storm do their work. Anxiety and care can never be quite absent. They are hardly more absent to-day than ever they were; only the day is sure to come in the nation as in our life, in our life as in the nation, when the flower unfolds to the sun in its perfect glory.

When the battle of Shiloh was fought, I went from Chicago to the battle-field, with a corps of nurses, to take care of the wounded men. Our city, when I left it, was sheeted in grim black weather: not a leaf was open on the trees, not a flower in the gardens. But, when we got into the South, the orchards were rejoicing in great rosy clouds of apple-blossom, and the woods were full of song. When I came back to Chicago, however, the trees were still bare. Here and there, a leaf had ventured out, and was shivering in the bitter wind: but there was no spring yet; and men were reaping up all their old grudges against the Lakes and their weather, and were sure the spring would never come.

Now, I have one tree just by my study window, with which I have managed to become very intimate. We nod to each other every morning. In those long black days, I could see my friend was looking disheartened enough. It had great treasure of buds; but it seemed to fold them as a child folds a treasure in its clasped fingers, and all the while to be saying, "Well, I do think this spring will never come." But I said, "Hold on, good tree: spring is coming. I saw her down there on the Alabama line. Here where you are is the winter, — fierce, persistent, determined to stay. Yonder, where I have been, is the spring, — soft, sunny, filling the woods with her white splendor; and I can see the blossoms pouring up this way, faster than I could run on my feet to tell you." And it was so. The warm days came at last; the summer was victor; and my tree stood, tremulous in her beautiful green robes, like a bride adorned for her wedding.

Now, why will men not take these things into their hearts, and be as full of faith in the meaning and purpose of their lives as of their flowers? Is the man alone the neglected step-child? are his fortunes alone misfortunes? are we much worse than the lilies? Or is it not of all things true, that as man rises nearest of all on this earth to the image of the Infinite, so he is nearest of all on this earth to the Providence that enfolds and blesses all?

II.

WHAT A LEAF SAID.

ISA. lxiv. 6: "We all do fade as a leaf."

MY text is a sermon in itself. It was whispered from the trees, as you came to church: it will rustle under your feet, as you go home. It is the sermon of these autumn days, proclaiming the dissolution, as the spring proclaimed the resurrection and the life. I heard this sermon, when I was seventeen, in the plane-trees that covered the foss of an old Roman camp: I shall hear it, if I live, when I am seventy, in the elms and maples by this lake shore; and it has always been the one thing, that the fading and falling leaf is the mute monitor of the fading and failing life.

And I can well believe how my experience must answer to yours, — how, in pensive moments all your life long, when the crimson banners unfold on the trees, and the leaves begin to fall about your path, you have thought more painfully of the fading life than at any other time in the year. This seems to be not only the common feeling, but the habit also of the prophet and seer. Few psalms were ever sung about the fading leaf, that had for their burden a great cry of accomplishment and victory. All rejoice over the purple grape and ripened grain. The fruit, ruddy and golden, seems to laugh at us on the tree; but the leaf, rustling under our feet or shivering in the sharp frost, seems to tell only of dissolution and death. We thank God in our great Thanksgiving for the kindly *fruits* of the earth: we never thank him for the kindly leaves. Every thing on the farm and in the garden is considered, except the leaf. " How strange and awful the gusty wind and whirling leaves of the autumnal day!" Coleridge cries; and he does but express what all men feel. We tack it into a distich for our children's copy-books; we set it to music, and sing it in our parlors, and churches; and we engrave it on the memorial stones of our dead,— that we all do fade as a leaf.

And yet I do not intend to re-echo this cry

to you this morning. At the best, it is not the cry of the gospel, but of the law. It is not of salvation by grace, but of dissolution by nature, that we are thinking, when the leaves flutter down from the trees, and the hollow winds sigh through the woodlands. He is no gospel minister who will wilfully discourse of discouragement. I know of no voice that ought to be held so sacredly for inspiration as the voice of the preacher, except, indeed, that of the husband or wife. We do not come to church to be told that we are withered leaves and crawling worms, but to be assured that we are men made only a *little* lower than the angels, and heirs of the everlasting life. We come to the preacher to hear what will help us sing, — to realize what there is beside and better than fading and falling. There is not a man of us that does not encounter quite enough on week-days to dishearten and discourage him, in being compelled to listen to " Thus saith the world," without being discouraged on a Sunday by " Thus saith the Lord."

So, while I will frankly say my text is true, and the sermon it preaches is true, and the whisper we hear in the autumn wind is true, this question still waits to be answered, "*How* is it true?" Is the fading of the leaf the only true thing about it, the only matter worth our painful, earnest thought; or is there something more and better? What can the leaf crimsoning on the tree, and the wind wailing through the branches, whisper to our hearts beside this one sad strain, "We all do fade as a leaf"?

Well, this, I think, first of all. It can say, "Take care you do not go wrong, in the first step, by misunderstanding entirely what it is for a leaf to fade; that you do not exalt that into the greatest, which may be of the smallest possible consequence; and that your steady gaze at this point in its being does not shut out at once reflection and anticipation, — what the leaf has been, and what it may be, in the providence of God."

I do not say this to apologize for the leaf. I have no idea that prospect and retrospect shall clasp hands over it, and hide it from our sight. I want the leaf to testify for itself, and say, "Yes, indeed, your text is true. I am a fading leaf certainly, — and all leaves fade. But then you must remember, that this is the true time to fade, as the May-days were to spring; and, I cannot doubt this, that any true time must be a good time. Beside, I want you to tell me, whether I am not, in my degree, a ripe and perfect fruit, as certainly as your grape or apple; and so whether my falling is not like the fall of all ripe fruit, the proof that I have done God's will through storm and shine, and hear him whispering, 'Well done' in the first frost; so that when I am turning to fall, am I not also turning to rise; to be again, in my degree, a servant and minister of the grace of God?

"The truth is," my leaf may continue, "you look at a leaf as you look at life, along the surface, instead of into the deep: your estimate is by superfice, not cube measure. I seem to fall: I do fall. But, if it were possible for you to see what I am doing beside, you would wonder, as you noted, how the spirit that has animated me, and been the life of my life, through all the days and nights since I came into being, is quietly freeing itself from its old familiar frame; and rising, not in fable but in fact, in deed and in truth, to wait the bidding of the Master; while the frame itself, this thing shivering over your head

or rustling under your feet, will be guarded and
kept until the morning of its resurrection. Did
you rejoice this summer over your strawberries
and roses, and not remember, how, for a thousand
ages, my race, faded leaves as you call us, have
lain treasured, waiting to be their ministers and
yours whenever you should come to need us?
You preach from your text, 'We all do fade as a
leaf:' why do you not sometimes preach from
that other text, 'The leaves of the tree are for
the healing of the nations?' What nation is not
healed through our ministry? What great thing
was ever done where we cast no shadow? You
cry 'Nothing but leaves,' and think you have
touched the dusty heart of all barrenness. When
you know what it is to be even a faded and
fallen leaf, there will be a better music in your
cry. It is true, we are nothing but leaves; yet,
in the order of the creation, you had been noth-
ing but for us. Here, as everywhere, there is no
broken link in the chain that binds all things
God has made, fast to his throne, no step lost
out of the ladder stretching from earth to heaven,
no dry place in the river of life. From the atom
to the angel, in Him we live and move, and have

our being; and he is not far from every one of us."

Then, when we come to understand this, we are aware how this leaf falls honorably, after doing what one leaf may do for its own and the common blessing. A mere leaf, one in countless myriads, it did not come out of chance, and does not go into chance. It cannot fall to the ground, as it could not bloom on the tree, without the will of our Father; and so, for leaves at least, whatever we may believe of lives, this fading and falling is not defeat and death, but victory and life.

For, again, if my leaf may testify, it will say, "I am a fading leaf certainly; watching for the sun and frost to give the signal for my dissolution. I have had to bear heavy rains, to wrestle with great storms, to shudder in electric fires, to fight my way and hold my own as well as I could in the teeth of foes and parasites, ever since I began to spring. But this I can say, as I fall, that there has been no day since I first began to grow, when I have not tried to be true to the law of my life, as the mediator, bridging the gulf between senseless matter and the sentient soul.

You rejoice in your fruit; if there had been no leaf, there could have been no fruit, and there would be no tree. The servant of all, I am, in my way, the greatest of all, by the infallible ordination and law of all service. I give you walnut for your gun-stock, and ash for the handle of your plough. I work through all weathers to build your ships, factories, homes, and churches. I am indispensable to the match for your fire, and the mast for your merchantman. I brace myself, and stand shoulder to shoulder with my fellows on great pines, keeping watch and ward in the long winter, on every coigne of vantage, to keep you from the driving northern storms, and spread myself as a shield over valley and champaign, to shelter you from the burning summer heats. I cast my mantle over the raindrop, until it can find a runlet; and the runlet I shelter to the rivulet, the rivulet to the river, and the river to the sea. I cover the springs among the moss, and weave my tapestry to adorn the bare desolation of the mountains. I hold myself, simple and separate, always to my one purpose. And now, in my falling, I shall fall for blessing, and cease to be a leaf because, as a leaf,

I am no longer needed. But, in ceasing to be what I am, I may well remind you of what one has said who loves us, and takes us into his heart beyond all men living: 'We compare ourselves to leaves: the leaves may well scorn the comparison, if we live only *for* ourselves. If ever in the autumn a pensiveness steals over us, as the leaves flutter by in their fading, may we not wisely look up to their mighty monuments; and as we see how fair they are, how far prolonged in arch and aisle the avenues of the valleys, the fringes of the hills, so stately, so eternal; the joy of man, the comfort of all living creatures, the glory of the earth — remember that these are but the monuments of fading leaves, that faintly flit past us to die? Let them not die before we read and understand their holy revelation; so that we also, careless of a monument for the grave, may build one in the world, by which men may be taught to remember, not where we died, but where we lived.'"

Then, keeping still to my parable, I can see how my leaf will say further: "You can think as you like, therefore, about man, as he fades and falls, — make the end of your life here as mournful as you please,—dishonor death by evil names and images, as its shadow falls upon your race; but I ask you, once for all, to leave me out of your sad analogies. I protest against being counted as one that shudders at dissolution. I might have done that in June, when my life was all to live; but in September, when it has had its day, as I begin to loosen from the spray where God caused me to spring, the loosening seems as good as ever did the springing.

"Then, there is another thing. I cannot tell much about it; it is just a sweet, misty mystery, to be made clear, no doubt, in due time. But near my heart, through all my summer, faint at first, but growing stronger with the growing days, I have felt and nursed and shielded the intimation of another springing in a spring-time to come, to which my present dissolution seems to be entirely indispensable. So, then, I shall die as I have lived, with my face to the sun and the great loving heavens, and welcome the autumn frost as I welcomed the spring sunshine. It is true that I have no hope like that your race holds of living again,—

> 'Wrapped from the fickle and the frail,
> With gathered powers yet the same,
> Piercing the keen seraphic flame
> From orb to orb, from vail to vail.'

My spirit must go whence it came, and my frame must be trodden into the dust; yet I fear nothing that can happen to either, because I know that both will be held in the hollow of His hand who counts a faded leaf. I am sure of all the life I shall ever need. I know that *my* Redeemer liveth. God will not leave *me* in the grave. Though I am only a leaf, 'All the days of my appointed time will I wait till *my* change come, and trust the wisdom that has done so well for me this time, what that change shall be.' And so, if men are crying, 'We all do fade as a leaf,' in any spirit of down-looking sadness and fear, let them speak for their race, not for ours; because, being true to life, we find out how to be true to death, and secure an entrance into the life to come."

Now, need 1 say, that, in lingering so over the leaf, I am seeking the lesson for the life, how sure is the assurance, that, if we will be so faithful even as a leaf on a tree, when we fade and fall there can be no room for regret; because

aspect, prospect, and retrospect will be all alike
good, as we look down into the deeps of life,
and up through its altitudes, instead of watching, as we do, merely along its surfaces. In
this spirit, I want to trace, then, the lesson of
my parable, pointed alike at the cry in the text
and the echo in our hearts. And, in doing this,
to keep as close as I can to the lines I have
drawn, and, running them along their natural
parallels of the leaf and the life, say agreed that
we all do fade as a leaf: what then?

For there is no alternative but to face the
fact. We all do fade and fall. We know that
dear faces and presences do fade out from every
life. I walked one summer under the green
leaves, on Staten Island, with as dear a friend
as ever man had on the earth; and we said,
"We will meet here, and walk and talk so,
every summer;" but, when we met again, something had changed. When the summer came
again, my friend was fighting for his life; and,
before another summer, I went down from the
West into the quiet New-England valley where
he was brought up, to say a prayer by his grave.
Indeed, indeed, it is true we all do fade as a leaf.

Yet I say, what then? Am I sure that I fully realize what it is to fade as a leaf? Do I touch, in my estimate, the cube or the superfice? Is it not true that, in my painful and steady gaze at this thing, I shut out both reflection and anticipation, and forget, that, with an assurance as much deeper as I am more than the leaf, I may be sure, that what I call fading and falling in is also ripening and gathering; and the time for the true life to be gathered, whenever it may be, is that life's October, and as divine in its way as the May was for its spring?

Because this truth is one with a vaster; namely, that not one aspect in life ought to fill my sight to the exclusion of another, but life altogether must be seen as we watch men fade and fall. "All leaves are builders," says Ruskin; "but they are to be divided into two orders,— those that build by the sword, and those that build by the shield." I would see every life as that most perfect of all seers into leaf-life sees every leaf. It may be that our lives are the most obscure and powerless for good this earth ever bore on her breast: I tell you, if we are trying to be what we can be, then the life of every one of us casts its speck of grateful shadow somewhere, holds itself somehow up to the sun and rain, fights its way with some poor success against storm and fire and foe and parasite; or it stands sternly, in these great days, shoulder to shoulder with its comrades, a strong tower of defence, to guard what we have won in our war for humanity, resolute not to fall into that trap the devil always sets for a generous people, of giving up in the treaty what they won in the fight. For it is true, and truest of all, that not the things which satisfy the world's heart easily; not purple grape, and golden apple, and ripe grain, and brown seed, and roses and asters; not the noble and beautiful, over which men rejoice and are glad,—are alone the fruit on the tree of life; but the leaf, faded, ragged and unnoticed, is fruit too; falling, when its day is done, it falls honorably; dying, it dies well; its work well done, and the world is better by the measure of what one poor leaf may do for its life.

All honor to the great men who so patiently and steadily broke through the triple armor that guarded the heart of the rebellion; sprang over the fastnesses of Georgia to paralyze its right

hand, and swept bareheaded through the broken
ranks of our men, shouting our battle-cry so
grandly, that they went storming back like a
whirlwind when they heard it, and wrenched
a victory out of the very jaws of defeat! And
honor to the man whose heart was quiet in
the dreadful days of the Wilderness, when only
a quiet heart and a mighty, with God's great
blessing, could avail us! Above all, honor to
the great, steady soul, whose counsel guided,
whose truth moulded, whose devotion sanctified,
and whose life and death made glorious, the land
that had given him birth, and honored him, and
elected him to the greatest place a man can fill!
These men, and all like them, are fruit. Let
their names be said and sung in every loyal heart
and home, and written in letters of living light
for men to read in the ages to come.

Ay, but I know of others as good and true.
Leaves, nothing but leaves. They were swept
down in the storms of battle, they withered in
the swamps and the sun, they faded out of our
homes and are dead; or they live and strive,
casting their shield, standing close, working the
work of Him that sent them. All honor to

the common soldier, the common laborer, the poor teacher, the man and woman everywhere, unknown and yet well known, — with no name to live, but bearing, in all they are and all they do, the assurance of the life everlasting! For as every leaf on every tree is, by the tenure of its life, a mediator and saviour, standing between the hard rock and living man, the bridge between life and death, — so this unknown man or woman, this common soldier or common worker, is fruit, in being leaf and falling, scorched by battle-fires or chilled by night damps; or, dying, worn out by toiling in the field of the world. Not one such man or woman has lived and striven and died in vain. There may be no monument to tell how they died or where they rest; but what they have done is their monument. The leaves of their tree are for the healing of the nations.

Mother, you think the little one that was taken from you could be nothing to the world; it faded so soon. Be sure, the leaf that lives only for a day is something to the tree; it has not lived in vain. This had been a poorer world, had any leaf of a day never bloomed; and so your little child has not only made you a richer woman than you possibly could have been had it never been born, but its touch of bloom has helped the world to bloom. It did not fall, as it could not spring, without the will of our Father; and, if you did but know it, its autumn was as true as its spring, and both were included in its few brief moments of life.

And this is the way the lesson of the leaf comes home to us all. We see about us other lives, noble and fruitful; and say, "If I could only do as that man or woman is doing; if I could accomplish some great thing that would be a world's wonder and blessing,—then, I think, I could die gladly. But the Master comes, seeking fruit and finding none. I plod on at my desk; I work in my home; I weary at my task, —unknown, unnoticed, unprofitable, and nobody." Well, my friend, I think discontent is as good a thing in its place as life has in its treasury. If you are young, there is probably hope for you in something like the measure of your discontent; and, if you are not young, that discontent is always good which can bring you into a larger activity. I know not but it is good to be always a little discontented. It is a sign, as when the dove fluttered to the window of the ark, that there are olive leaves outside for the plucking. Still, I tell you, the question for most of us to solve is not, Am I fruit? but Am I a leaf? I take it, if we are to be fruit, we shall be by some deep predestination; and what we shall have to do in that case will be to keep as sound as we can to the core. But, if I am not fruit, then I am leaf; and leaf is fruit in its own order. Do I cast a mite of shadow; do I beautify ever so small a piece of blank barrenness; do I help along, in the measure of my one-leaf power, in forming, if not fruit, then timber? because, this question answered right, I have answered every other.

Let me make this sure; and then I may be sure of this also, that the nipping frosts of the autumn, when they come, will be as divine to me as the dewy splendors of June. A falling leaf, I shall fall honorably; and the spirit, returning to the God who gave it, will again be set to do the greatest, and by consequence the most blessed, thing it can do; while this frame, the faded leaf, will wait for the morning of its resurrection. For this corruptible shall put on incorruption, and this mortal immortality. And when a man reaches this faith, he will not fear death any more than he fears life: —

"Fear death! to feel the fog at my throat,
   The mist on my face,
When the snows begin, and the blasts denote
   I am nearing the place;
The power of the night, the press of the storm,
   The post of the foe, —
Where he stands, the arch fear, in a visible form,
   And the strong man must go!
No; let me feel all of it; fare like my peers
   Who have met him of old;
Bear the brunt; in a moment pay life's whole arrears
   Of pain, darkness, and cold:
For sudden the worst turns the best to the brave.
   The dark minutes at end,
Then the elements rage; and the voices that rave
   Shall soften and blend,—
Shall change, and become,
   First a peace, then a joy, then thy breast.
O thou soul of my soul, I shall meet thee again,
   And with God be the rest!

III.

THE TREASURES OF THE SNOW.

MEDITATING through the week what I should say to you to-day, my mind at last began to turn steadily toward the snow that was falling all day long between the window where I sat and my church, covering the city with its white robe to be instantly soiled and torn, and casting an unspotted radiance over hundreds of miles of the land through which also it was my lot to travel. So I gradually became aware, that to-day I must speak to you about the snow, and its place in the world and life in which we are now witnessing its presence, — see what hint of the Divine blessing is revealed to us in this fair vesture of the winter, — the delight of our youth, the touching image of the white age before the opening of a new spring, and the fair shroud, that, in the black winter days, covers all the graves.

I read a story once of what had happened just before in one of the new English colonies. It was a land where the snow fell but seldom. The children had grown up to a good age, without once seeing it. One day, the thick flakes began to fall; the children were terrified; they shrank back from it, — did not know what to make of it: but the parents ran out to welcome what it was the first impulse of the children to fear. The unknown wonder of the one was the welcome visitor of the other, bringing hosts of kindly memories. It melted as it fell, was what we now watch with disgust on sloppy days, and call neither one thing nor the other. But, as these men and women saw the feathery fleece falling for the first time in their new home on the other side of the world, it seemed to bring the blessing of the old home on its wings, to make their past and present more intimately one. It was a means of grace to them: it came down cold out of the heavens; but their hearts became all aglow, as it touched them.

I had written as far as this, when a lady came to my study, and I read the incident to her. — "I know something as good as that," she said. "I had a friend who went south, out of the reach of the snow, lived there many years, and then came north again. When the first snow fell after her return, she ran out to meet it with all the delight of a child, caught a flake in her hand, and kissed it." A flake in her hand to kiss, — she could not resist the impulse. It was an old friend she had nearly forgotten, as welcome as the flowers in May. The philosopher could tell her, to be sure, that this was not the snow that used to fall about the old homestead. She knew better: it was the same snow, because she was the same woman: the identity was in her own nature. It was a hint of that better life to come, in which we are not to reckon by then and now, by past and present, — what was, and is not, and never can be again; but by an eternal now, fresh and full as the heart of a great ocean.

It is notable that there is but one instance of an actual snow-fall in the Bible; and even that is rather a recollection than a record. It is in the Second Book of Samuel, where, speaking of a mighty man, the chronicler says he slew a lion in the midst of a pit, in the time of snow. If the man and the lion were in the pit together, it was a fine piece of valor; but if it was done as the same thing is done now in Africa, where a pit is dug into which the lion falls and then is killed from above, one cannot but think, that the lion might have had more to say about it, had the thing been done on the open plain and in warm weather. In the poetry of the elder Scriptures, the references to the snow are far more thick-strewn than in the histories, showing how the presence of the white glory melted into the souls of those most open to all the influences of heaven, summer and winter alike. "Hast thou entered into the treasures of the snow?" the Almighty is made to ask impatient Job. And Job himself uses the term three times, always, however, in the sense of melting or melted snow, as if the man had not come into actual contact with it, but had seen it, as I saw it, melting and pouring from the mountains in Switzerland under the August sun. In the Psalms there is an exquisite hint of a snow-fall through the perfect stillness, and a magnificent storm piece into which the snow comes with other elements. In the Proverbs, again, there is a passage, how that there is nothing new under the sun, in the matter of ice-cold drinks in summer, where the writer says, "As the cold of snow in the time of harvest, so a faithful servant refreshes the soul of his master;" from which we may also infer, that even Solomon, in all his glory, had trouble with his servants. Isaiah has a noble image of the truth falling softly and fruitening the heart, as the snow falls and fruitens the earth. There is not a word about the snow from the lips of the Saviour; and it is only noticed at all in the New Testament in a secondary sense, — used as a comparison, never as an experience.

But to men that dwell, as we do, where the snow is our constant companion through a long winter, there is both opportunity and necessity to enter more deeply into its meaning, than any men have ever done who have only seen it at second-hand, crowning Hermon with its radiance, and lying white in the ravines of Lebanon. We can see, if we will, how there is that in it which at once illustrates the law, supplements the gospel, and reveals the Almighty as intimately and wonderfully present in the snows of winter as in the blossoms of spring, or the greenery of summer, or the gold of the autumn of the year. When John Foster learned that snow had been detected on the poles of Mars, the white light of it growing large in what must be the planet's winter, and then small again in his summer, it made him very sad. He argued, that the presence of the snow meant cold; cold, suffering; suffering, sin; and sin, on another planet,— a frightful extension of the curse and fall. It made him sad, because, great man as he was, he lived in the belief that this fair world was wrecked and ruined in the biting of an apple; that a man and woman, as inexperienced as two babies, were placed in a position to do a mischief for which I am at a loss to find a comparison. I thought of myself as placing my five-year-old boy on the locomotive of a great train, and giving him the lever, with a strong temptation to turn it, and a strict command to let it alone; then leaving him to his own devices, and the passengers to their doom. But the illustration is too feeble to convey the idea of the common doctrine of the Fall. It was the man's misfortune, that, otherwise so great and good, he could permit his soul to be bolted fast in a prison so dark, that the very stars in heaven were no better to him than a great penitentiary and graveyard.

"There is no such thing in nature as bad weather," James Hogg used to say; and certainly he got his share of all the weathers possible to the bleak moorlands of Scotland: and Coleridge said, "In nature there is nothing melancholy." And both philosopher and shepherd, in saying such things, touched the brighter and better belief, dawning now on the world in the liberal faith. That the snow was on Hermon when Adam was in Eden before the Fall,— did not come for a curse there or anywhere, but a blessing; not to work ruin on the snow-line of Ararat, any more than on the wheat-fields of Wisconsin; and is as innocent of our sins, this way or that, as the white robe of an angel. And so the whole drift of our discovery of the nature of the snow, is at the same time a revelation of its grace and goodness.

I look out of my window at the whirling tempest, or set my face against it grimly on the street, or see it descending and covering a hundred leagues of wintry land; and shudder, if I am in a shuddering mood, and say, "God help the poor!" and am, perhaps, content enough to let God help them, as I creep back into my own snug nest. But, while I am sheltering there, let me take Scoresby's book on the Arctic Regions, or Glaisher's book on the Snow, and watch, to my endless wonder, what beauty is in a snow-flake.

That is not a rack of whirling wintry chaos I see!—the churning of wind and water and frost into a white fury; the desolation of a world in which God is not. There is not an atom of snow in this whole wide belt of the storm that is not in itself a gem of exquisite outline and inline, not any two of those innumerable myriads of flakes alike, and yet they all dart out into the same wonderful six-rayed glory. I may grind them, if I can, into a more impalpable powder than this into which they are crushed in these roaring mills of God; then put the smallest atom under my microscope; and, if I can get one fair glance at it, I will still see the perfect unlike sixfold likeness, no more, no less, as inexhaustible in its loveliness as the power that made it. So the flakes call to us for ever through the moan and shriek of the storm, or whisper as they fall in silence, and rest on the land like wool, "Hast thou entered into the treasures of the snow?" And tell us how the revelation of the microscope chords with the words of the Master, about the robing of a lily, that, down to the minutest and most common thing, the hand of their Maker and our Father reaches, as perfectly as up to the most celestial and divine. It is disorder to us; it is order to him. He directs the storm. Snow and hail, fire and vapor, and stormy wind, fulfil his word. Not a sparrow or a snow-flake falleth to the ground without the will of your Father. I ask the star, as it melts on my hand, "What proof can you give me that you are not born of the mere spume of the tempest?" It looks at me from beneath its six-rayed crown, and answers, "I am no more that than the Atlantic. I come out of order and light, a child of the day. I am on the Lord's side. I come from heaven, as the good angels come, to assure you afresh of its immanence, and help you to enter in and be saved."

Then this beauty chords again with the blessing of the snow. In great cities we think little of snow, except as it brings good sleighing or evil walking, or the threat of the policeman if we do not clean our sidewalks, or thin congregations, or discomfort to our feet, or irregular mails and trains. Indeed I doubt whether the snow was ever meant for the city. It is as thoroughly out of contrast in it as a stray lamb, and has no more power to hold its white fleece whole, and live on our streets. But, in the country, we instantly find what this means: "He giveth snow like wool." Between the surface of the earth and the surface of the snow, the measured difference in temperature is sometimes forty degrees. It is always welcome in these latitudes, when it comes early and in plenty, and stays well on the land; for then the farmer knows that the things will be happed away snug and warm, that must survive the winter. In the Lake-Superior region, much colder than our own, — where the snow falls with the first frosts, and stays to the edge of summer, — many of the plants we dig up, and put into our cellars, are left in the ground with perfect safety, because "He giveth snow like wool" to preserve them under its warm fleece. In my readings, I have found many curious records of persons buried under the snow, surviving through long spans of time; but, if a hand or a foot was exposed, that was lost.

When I was at Fort Donelson, and there heard that grand story, how the Iowa Second went over the ramparts, and stayed, sleeping all night in the snow, my informant said, "I looked along the line where I knew they must be next morning; but all I could see was a row of white mounds, out of which they rose presently, shaking the snow from their blankets, and resuming order of battle."—"And was it not a fearful thing to lie under that covering?" I said to one of the men afterward. "Well," he replied, "it wasn't quite so warm as some places I have slept in: still it was not at all so bad as you imagine."

The snow is, in its measure, the power of God unto salvation. It is not an aggravation of winter, but a defence against it. Philosophy blends with science to tell of its grace and goodness. We talk to our children of the good fairies, in which, alas for them! they believe no more than we do. We might do better, if we told them the truth about such a thing as the snow,—how God sends, in the snow-flakes, a guardian angel for every grass-blade and flower-seed he will keep from the frost, to protect them first, and then to sink into their hearts, and rise with them in the morning of their resurrection. And then I would try to see what I taught, — the goodness of God in a snow-storm. It is something to see, for one hour, a snow-driven city, — to admire how all the vileness is hidden for a few minutes out of sight, though there were no use except that in it. But, in the country, the snow casting its white robe of protection over the land, —gathering it as a hen gathereth her chickens under her wings, — that is a sight which leads us again toward the heaven out of which the wonder comes. And so I would touch these snow-flakes less for what they prove than for what they are, — the testimony of a snow-drift to the Sermon on the Mount; the extension of Christ's great argument out of summer into winter. If God so shape the snow-star, can he fail finally to shape the soul? and if he giveth snow like wool, to hap the shivering seed; if he so clothe the land as well as the lily, — will he leave me naked?

But then I can see how the blessing of the snow comes home still more nearly and directly.

It is good to watch the snow, as I have tried to do; to note —

> "The tiny spherule traced with lines
> Of nature's geometric signs;"

and what an exact order and harmony is at the heart of the endless agitation of a snow-storm; and to realize something of the blessing that comes when "He giveth snow like wool." But there is a better blessing in the snow, that can come to us all, though we never saw a microscope or snow book, and know of the thing only as something thoroughly identified with winter.

"I think better of snow-storms," Prescott says, "since I find, that, though they keep a man's body indoors, they bring his mind out." It has been said by another, that, while the land is more fruitful as you approach the tropics, what is taken out of the land is put into the man as you touch the snow. In Iceland, where they are shut out from the rest of the world through the greater part of the year, and —

> "The housemates sit
> Around the radiant fireplace, enclosed
> In a tumultuous privacy of storm," —

there has been a separate, and in its way quite a noble, scholarship, to which we owe the preservation of some of the most precious Sagas, fragments of the earliest history of our own race. If you will draw a line from Edinburgh southward until it touches just half-way in the measured distance of England and Scotland together, and then count the greatest names in each half for a long time back now,—Burns, Scott, Wordsworth, Watt, Arkwright, and the Stephensons, with others more than I can mention,—you will see, that, though London and the Universities are to the south of the line, the preponderance of genius and power is to the north; especially in those priceless instances of men who had to cleave their way upward out of the forge, coal-pit, and hungry farm-lands, to fame.

In our own country, this fact is still more striking and clear. Whatever line can live in our literature, so far has been written in the North. The most precious fruits in all the higher departments of life and learning have ripened within the snow-line. Nay, it is remarkable, that in the thin edge of land between Cincinnati or St. Louis and our own city, there is this difference, that, in the gravest times this nation has ever known, the great ballads, whose influence for good was incalculable, — ballads like the " Battle-cry of Freedom," — came from the city that is set farthest in the snow. I mention these instances as hints of what I mean by that better blessing in the snow than the contemplation of its starry order and noble uses as it lies on the land. What every healthy man and woman feels, when, after the disheartening rains of the last weeks in the autumn, the first powder of the white blessing falls ; and then, as winter deepens, the snow comes in good earnest, and —

> " The whited air
> Hides hills and woods, the river and the heaven," —

that is the intimation of the difference between the snow present in, and absent from, our life.

So when I hear letters read from friends in the South, that tell how, while we are battling with the snow, they are enjoying the roses, I say, " Well, the rose had to come out of the snow. It is not a native and natural denizen of the southern, but of the northern, hemisphere." That is true for one thing. And then we *shall* have the roses, and we have the snow. Those dwellers in summer lands have the one blessing ; we have both. What can they do when the ques tion is asked of them, "Hast thou entered into the treasures of the snow?" but stand silent and conscious of their poverty, if they will but have the grace? For, not to dwell on that hearty and healthful recreation, only possible to a few of the dwellers in cities,—the pleasantness of sweeping through the snow in sleighs and good company, a means of grace by no means to be despised, providing always that the termination of your ride be not a tavern,—not to dwell on this, I say, the man whose lot is cast where the roses bloom outdoors in January might well exchange his roses for the final blessing that comes hidden in the snow.

When, on the edge of a wild winter night, the snow begins to come down thick and fast, darkening the heavens, covering the earth, muffling all sounds, foiling all sights; when the children rush home from school, and the father from business, and the shutters are fastened, and the curtains are drawn, and the supper is done, and the clear, open, wood or soft-coal fire is made up,— for one or the other of these I consider entirely indispensable to a right study of the treasures of the snow,—and all sit in the sweet light

together, and try to remember one sick or poor
for whom they have not done what they could,
but are utterly unable; and the books are brought
out, and the work, which, to be seasonable at
such a time, should be just as good as play;
and there is cheerful chat among the elders of
far-away times, and prophecy among the youth
of what shall be, to be fulfilled as God will and
as they will; while still the snow falls and beats
about the home, and hisses down into the fire;
and the heart grows tender in its thankfulness,
reaching out into the very wilderness, and cry-
ing with Burns, —

> "Ilk happing bird, wee, helpless thing,
> That, in the merry months o' spring,
> Delighted us to hear thee sing, —
> What comes o' thee?
> Whaur wilt thou cower thy chittering wing,
> And close thy ee?" —

these, friends, are some of the treasures of the
snow, as they lie most obviously open to our rev-
erent study, inestimable, in their way, as the
blossoms of the spring, the flowers of the sum-
mer, and the fruit of the autumn of the year.

It might be expected that I should now make
an application: I have none to make. One thing

only I can touch of the deeper spirit, beside what I have touched as I have gone along. We speak of the snow as of an image of death. It may be that; but it hides the everlasting life always under its robe, — the life to be revealed in due time, when all cold shadows shall melt away before the ascending sun, and we shall be, not unclothed, but clothed upon, and mortality shall be swallowed up of life.

Jan. 26, 1867.

IV.

LIGHT ON A HIDDEN WAY.

Job iii. 23: "Why is light given to a man whose way is hid?"

"THE Book of Job," says Thomas Carlyle, " is one of the grandest things ever written with a pen ; our first statement, in books, of the problem of the destiny of man, and the way God takes with him on this earth ; grand in its simplicity and epic melody, sublime in its sorrow and reconciliation ; a choral melody, old as the heart of man, soft as the summer midnight, wonderful as the world with its seas and stars ; and there is no other thing in the Bible, or out of it, of equal literary merit." It is not possible now to tell whether the book is a real history, or a sort of oriental drama. The question is one that will always keep the critics hard at work, so long as there are rational, and what ought in all fairness to be called not rational, schools in theology. My own idea is, that the rude outline of the history was floating about the desert, as the history of Lear or Macbeth floated about in later times among our own fore-elders; that, like those great dramas, it was taken into the heart of some man now forgotten, and came out again endowed with this wondrous quality of inspiration and life, that will bear it onward through all time. But, whatever the truth may be in this direction, this is clear, that, when Job put the question I have taken for a text, he was as far down in the world as a man can be who is not abased by sin. He had been the richest man in the country, honored by all that knew him, for his wisdom, his goodness, or his money. He was now so poor, that he says, men derided him whose fathers he would not have set with the dogs of his flock. He had been a sound, healthy man, full of human impulses and activities; had been sight to the blind, feet to the lame, a father to the poor, a defender of the oppressed. He was now a diseased and broken man, sitting on the ashes of a ruined home; his fires all gone out; his household gods all shattered; his children all dead; and his wife, the mother of his ten children, lost to the mighty love which will take ever so delicate but true-hearted woman at such a time, and make her a tower of strength to the man. His wife — who should have stood, as the angels stand, at once by his side and above him — turned on him in his uttermost sorrow, and said, " Curse God, and die."

Two things, in this sad time, seem to have smitten Job with most unconquerable pain. First, he could not make his condition chord with his conviction of what ought to have happened. He had been trained to believe in the axiom we put up in our Sunday schools, that to be good is to be happy. Now he *had* been good, and yet here he was as miserable as it was possible for a man to be. And the worst of all was, he could not deaden down to the level of his misery. The light given him on the divine justice would not let him rest. His subtle spirit, piercing, restless, dissatisfied, tried him every moment. Questions like these came up in his mind : " Why have I lost my money? I made it honestly, and made good use of it. Why is my home ruined? I never brought upon it one shadow of disgrace. Why am I bereaven of my children, and worse than bereaven of my wife? If this is the result of goodness, where is cause and effect? What is there to hold on by, if all this misery and mildew can come of upright, downright truth and purity?" Questions like these forced themselves upon him, and would not be silenced. There was but one way in which they could have been silenced. If this spirit that troubled him could have whispered, "Now, Job, what is the use of your whining? You know that you have got just what you deserve ; that you are a poor, old pewter Pecksniff, with not one grain of real silver about you. Your whole life has been a sham. You have said, —

> 'No graven images may be worshipped,
> Save in the currency;
> Thou shalt not kill, but need not strive
> Officiously to keep alive;
> Thou shalt not covet, but tradition
> Approves all forms of competition.' "

If the spirit could have spoken so to the man, he must have been dumb under a sense of the justice of his punishment; but there was no such sense for him: his entire life had been a good life, and the very light on his life in the past made his present way only all the darker.

Then the second element in Job's misery seems to lie in the fact, that there appeared to be light

everywhere, except on his own life. If life would
strike a fair average; if other good men had
suffered too, or even bad men,—then he could
bear it better. But the world went on just the
same. The sun shone with as much splendor
as on his wedding-day. The moon poured out
her tides of molten gold, night fretted the blue
vault with fires, trees blossomed, birds sang,
young men and maidens danced under the palms.
Other homes were full of gladness. This man
had sold his clip for a great price: the light-
ning had slain Job's sheep. That man had done
well in dates: the tornado had twisted Job's trees
down. Nay, worst of all, here were *wicked* men,
mighty in wealth; *their* houses in peace, without
fear; *their* children established in their sight,—
sending forth little ones like a flock, spending
their days in prosperity, and yet saying, "Who
is the Almighty that we should fear him?" while
here he was, a poor wreck, stranded on a deso-
late shore; a broken man, crying, "Oh that it
were with me as in days gone by, when the can-
dle of the Lord shone round about me; when I
took my seat in the market-place, and justice was
my robe and diadem! When I think of it, I am

confounded. One dieth in the fulness of his prosperity, wholly at ease and quiet: another dieth in the bitterness of his soul, not having tasted pleasure. How is it? What does it mean? Why is light given to a man whose way is hid?"

Now I suppose that not many men ever fall into such supreme desolation as this, that is made to centre in the life of this most sorrowful man. "It is the possible of that which in itself is only positive." But then it is true that one may reach out in all directions, and find men and women who are conscious of the light shining, but who cannot find the way; whose condition will not chord with their conception of life; who, in a certain sense, would be better if they were not so good. The very perfection of their nature is the way by which they are most easily bruised. Keen, earnest, onward, not satisfied to be below their own ideal, they are yet turned so wofully this way and that by adverse circumstances, that, at the last, they either come to accept their life as a doom, and bear it in grim silence; or they cut the masts when the storm comes, and drift a helpless hull broadside to the breakers, to go down finally like a stone.

Here is a young man newly come to your city, fresh from his good country home. He is resolved to make a mark, — to be the best sort of a man. He is full of budding energies and capabilities. Let him once get hold fairly, and he is sure to succeed. But he finds it difficult to start: places are not plenty. It is very hard, uphill work: he strives, and stays poor. He does not find the way. At last he is hungry and faint in the wilderness, alone; and the Devil comes, tempting him. He is a very nice person probably, wears a good coat, lives in good style: it may be he has a pew in church. He says, "Here is something I want done: if you will do it, you will get what *you* want, the kingdom of the world. It is not what puritanic people call right, to be sure; but there is no harm in it. Everybody does it; and, if you do it, you are sure to succeed." That young man is in danger, just as his life rises in strong, fierce jets, and is full of latent power. If he take counsel of his impatience, he will kneel down there and then, and do as he is bid. And it is possible that he will get what he bargained for, but with this difference, that, while he stands fast in his integrity, though there is no way, the light shines; when he has once gone down, the way may be open, but the light is gone. Or he succeeds in all manly integrity, makes his fortune, and then gradually slides into a belief in a Providence like that Job believed in before his trouble came, — a Providence that will keep him prosperous, because he is a good man: a great crash comes, and he loses all, including his belief in God. Or he makes a fortune, and holds it, but then forgets that money to a man is like water to a plant, — only useful so long as it promotes growth. Like water in the fountain or water in the tank, keep it flowing, and it blesses; keep it stagnant, and it kills.

The maiden comes out of her home, with the bloom of youth on her soul, — a wonder of love and trust. She walks wistfully down the world, and gradually is aware, that she will never meet the man she can wed. Yet her heart is full of love, and there are moments when she feels very *very* sad, trying to reconcile her nature to her condition; and *she* cries, "Why is light given, when the way is hid?" Or she weds, believing that she has found a man sent from God for her, to find afterward, perhaps, that she is mistaken by half a diameter. Yet she will strive hard and long to see in him the man God has put into her heart, but will give it up at the last, and say, "Why is light given, when the way is hid?"

Or the man and woman are set each to each, like perfect music, unto noble words; but one is taken, and the other left. John Wilson, walking down the world with such a wife by his side, said, "I shall die in my nest: I shall see no sorrow." But, one morning, he stood before his class, and said, "Gentlemen, I have not examined your essays: I could not see to read them in the valley of the shadow of death where I have been;" and then the strong man bowed himself, and wept sore, and went to his darkened home.

Or the man and woman live in sweet accord; but their home is too quiet, or it ripples over with sweet laughter, and then passes again into silence.

Or here, in the larger life, is a prince and leader of men. The roots of his power begin to ramify through all the land. He seems to be the one indispensable man of the time. In the sorest need of all, he is smitten down, and dies.

Or here is a great cause, reaching back into a great principle. The light of the divine justice shines on the principle, and so wins men to it that they cannot rest. Year after year, they will stand suffering, toiling, dying for their cause; but the way does not open. Yet they cannot choose but follow the light. If the light had not shone so in our own land, we might have ground along in some sort of affinity to slavery. It was light poured on the conscience of the nation, that brought on the war; it was light shining through the darkness, that kept the nation steady. Had no such light shone, we should have constructed a new Union, with the shackle of the slave for a wedding-ring. But the light stood like a wall of fire: yet how long it was only a light shining on a hidden way! — our homes black with desolation; fathers, mothers, wives, only putting on a cheerful look, because they would not by their sadness dishearten the great heart of the nation.

And so, I say, in men and nations you will find everywhere this discord between the longing that is in the soul, and what the man can do. Our life, as some one has said of the Cathedral of Cologne, seems to be a broken promise made to God; and —

> "How blest we should be,
> We have always believed,
> Had we really achieved
> What we nearly achieved!
> The thought that most thrilled
> Our existence is one
> That before we could frame it
> In language is gone.
> The more we gaze up into heaven,
> The more do we feel our gaze fail.
> All attempts to explore,
> With earth's finite insight,
> Heaven's infinite gladness,
> Is baffled by something
> Like infinite sadness."

Now trying, secondly, to find some solution of this question, I want to say frankly, that I cannot pretend to make the mystery all clear, so that it will give you no more trouble; because I cannot put a girdle round the world in forty minutes, and because a full solution must depend greatly on our own dissolution. "Let the light enter," said the great German, and then — died. I believe, also, that the man who thinks he has left nothing unexplained, in the mystery of providence and life, has rather explained nothing. I listen to him, if I am in trouble; and then I go home, and break my heart all the same; because

I see that he has not only not cleared up the mystery, but that he does not know enough about it to trouble him. The "Principia" and the Single Rule of Three are alike simple and easy to him, because he does not know the Rule of Three. And so I cannot be satisfied with the last words which some later hand has added to the book that holds this sad history. They tell us how Job has all his property doubled, to the last ass and camel, — has seven sons again and three daughters, has entire satisfaction of all his accusers, lives a hundred and forty years, sees four generations of his line, and then dies — satisfied. Need I say that this solution will not stand the test of life; that if life, on the average, came out so from its most trying ordeal, there would be little need for sermons like this? For then every life would be an open, self-contained providence, and the last page in time would vindicate the first. Men do not so live and die; and such cannot have been the primitive conclusion of the history. It has deeper meaning and a sublimer justification, or it had never been inspired by the Holy Ghost.

And this is sure to suggest itself to you,

as you read the history, that Job, in his trouble, would have lost nothing and gained very much, if he had not been so hasty in coming to the conclusion, that God had left him, that life was a mere apple of Sodom, that he had backed up to great walls of fate, and that he had not a friend left on earth. His soul, looking through her darkened windows, concluded the heavens were dark. The nerve, quivering at the gentlest touch, mistook the ministration of mercy for a blow. He might have found some cool shelter for his agony: he preferred to sit on the ashes in the burning sun. He knew not where the next robe was to come from: this did not deter him from tearing to shreds the robe that was to shelter him from the keen winds. It was a dreadful trial at the best; it was worse for his way of meeting it; and, when he was at once in the worst health and temper possible, he said, "Why is light given to a man whose way is hid?" Is not this now, as it was then, one of the most serious mistakes that can be made? I try to solve great problems of providence, perhaps, when I am so unstrung as to be entirely unfitted to touch their more subtle, delicate, and far-reaching harmonics. As well might you decide on some exquisite anthem when your organ is broken, and conclude there is no music in it because you can make no music of it, as, in such a condition of the life and such a temper of the spirit, try to find these great harmonies of God. When I am in trouble, then, and darkness comes down on me like a pall, the first question ought to be, "How much of this unbelief about providence and life, like Cowper's sense of the unpardonable sin, comes from the most material disorganization? Is the darkness I feel *in* the soul, or is it on the windows through which the soul must see?" Then, clear on this matter, the man tried so will endeavor to stand at the first, where this sad-hearted man stood at the last, in the shadow of the Almighty, if he *must* stand in a shadow, and hold on to the confidence that somewhere within all this trial is the eternal, the shadow of a great rock in a weary land.

It is a wonderful story. Job and his friends speculate all about the mystery, and their conclusions from their premises are entirely correct; but they have forgotten to take in the separate sovereign will of God, as working out a great purpose in the man's life, by which he is to be lifted into a grander reach of insight and experience than ever he had before. Job said, "I suffer, I am in darkness and disappointment and pain, because it is fate." Job's friends said, "No: you suffer because you have sinned. Rushes never grow without mire." They were both wrong, and all wrong. He suffered because that was the divine way of bringing him out of his sleek, self-satisfied content; and when, through suffering, that was done, he said, "I have heard of Thee with mine ears, but now mine eye seeth thee." There is a bird, it is said, that will never learn the song his master will have him sing, while his cage is full of light. He listens, and learns a snatch of this, a trill of that, a polyglot of all the songs in the grove, but never a separate and entire melody of his own. But the master covers his cage, — makes the way all dark about him: then he will listen, and listen to the one song he has to sing; and try and try, and try again, until at the last his heart is full of it: then, when he has caught the melody, the cage is uncovered. When there is light on the song, there is no need for darkness on the way.

Friends, if I had never gone into darkened rooms, where the soul stands at the parting of the worlds; or sat down beside widows and little children, when the desire of their eyes was taken away with a stroke; or grasped the hands of strong men, when all they had toiled for was gone, — nothing left but honor; or ministered to men mangled on the battle-field, beyond all telling; and heard, in *all* these places where darkness was on the way, melodies, *melodies* that I never heard among the common-places of prosperity, — I could not be so sure as I am, that God often darkens the way that the melody may grow clear and entire in the soul.

Then, if this man could have known, — as he sat there in the ashes, bruising his heart on this problem of providence, — that, in the trouble that had come upon him, he was doing what one man may do to work out the problem for the world, he might again have taken courage. No man lives to himself. Job's life is but your life and mine, written in larger text. What we are all doing, as we stand in our lot, steady to our manliness or womanliness in our black days, is to tell, in its measure, on the life and faith of every

good man coming after us, though our name may
be forgotten. There is a story in the annals of
science touching this principle, that we cannot
struggle faithfully with these things, and leave
them as we found them. Plato, piercing here
and there with his wonderful Greek eyes, —

> "Searching, through all he felt and saw,
> The springs of life, the depths of awe,
> To reach the law within the law," —

was impressed by the suggestive beauty of the
elliptic figure. He tried to search out its full
meaning, but died without the sight. A century
and a half after Plato, Apollonius came, was
arrested in the same way, took up the question
where Plato left it, tried to find out its full mean-
ings, and died without the sight. "And so,"
says a fine writer recently, "for eighteen cen-
turies, some of the best minds were fascinated by
this problem, — drew from it strength and disci-
pline; and yet, in all this time, the problem was
an abstract form, a beautiful or painful specula-
tion." It did not open out into any harmonious
principle. There was light on the thing, but no
light on the way. In the full time, Kepler came;
sat down to the study; and by what we call the
suggestion of genius, but ought to call the inspi-

ration of the Almighty, found that the orbits of the planets were elliptical. He died. Then Newton was born, took up the problem where Kepler had laid it down, made all the established facts the base of his mightier labors; and, when he had done, he had shown that this figure, this problem, that had held men spellbound through the ages, is a prime element in the law of universal gravitation, — at once the most beautiful theory and the most absolute conclusion of science. Then men could see how it was, *because* God had made the light shine on the thing, that the way was found. From Newton back to Plato, in true apostolic order, every man, bending over this mystery of a light where there was no way, wrestling faithfully with it, had not only grown more noble in his own soul in the struggle, but had done his share toward the solution found by this greatest and last who was also " born under the law, that they might receive the adoption of sons."

So, I tell you, is this restless search for a condition that shall answer to our conception; this fascination, that compels us to search out the elliptic of providence, — the geometric certainty underlying the apparent eccentricity. And every struggle to find this certainty; every endeavor to plumb the deepest causes of the discord between what the nature bears and what the soul believes; every striving to find the God of our loftiest faith in our darkest day, will, in some way, aid the demonstration, until, in the full time, some Newton of the soul will come, and, gathering the result of all these struggles between our conception of life and our condition in life, will make it the base of some vast generalization, that will bring the ripest conclusions of the science of providence into perfect accord with the old, grand apostolic revelation, "We know that all things work together for good to them that love God." We wrong the deepest revelations of life, when we are not content to let this one little segment in the arc of our existence stand in its own simple, separate intention, whether it be gladness or gloom; and trust surely, if we are faithful, that the full and perfect intention must come out in the full range of our being.

God seldom, perhaps never, works out his *visible* purpose in one life: how, then, shall he in one life work out his perfect will? The dumb poetry in William Burns the father had to wait for Robert Burns the son. Bernardo waited to be perfected in his son Torquato Tasso; William Herschel left many a problem in the heavens for John Herschel to make clear; Leopold Mozart wrestled with melodies that Chrysostom Mozart found afterward singing of themselves in every chamber of his brain; and Raymond Bonheur needed his daughter Rosa to come, and paint out his pictures for him.

Dr. Reid has said, that, when the bee makes its cell so geometrically, the geometry is not in the bee, but in the geometrician that made the bee. Alas, if in the Maker there is no such order for us as there is for the bee! If God so instruct the bee; if God so feed the bird; if even the lions, roaring after their prey, seek their meat from God; if he not only holds the linnet on the spray, but the lion on the spring, — how shall we dare lose heart and hope?

So, then, while we may not know what trials wait on any of us, we can believe, that as the days in which this man wrestled with his dark maladies are the only days that make him worth remembrance, and but for which his name had never been written in the book of life; so the days through which we struggle, finding no way, but never losing the light, will be the most significant we are called to live. Indeed men in all ages have wrestled with this problem of the difference between the conception and the condition. Literature is full of these appeals, from the doom that is on us to the love that is over us, — from the God we *fear* to the God we *worship*. The very Christ cries once, " My God! why hast *thou* forsaken me?" Yet never did our noblest and best, our apostles, martyrs, and confessors, flinch finally from their trust, that God is light; that life is divine; that there is a way, though we may not see it; and have gone singing of their deep confidence, by fire and cross, into the shadow of death. It is true, nay, it is truest of all, that " men who suffered countless ills, in battles for the true and just," have had the strongest conviction, like old Latimer, that a way would open in those moments when it seemed most impossible. Their light on the *thing* brought a commanding assurance, that there must somewhere, sometime, be light on the *way*.

"I say to thee, do thou repeat
To the first man that thou shalt meet
In lane, highway, or open street, —

That he and we, and all men, move
Under a canopy of love
As broad as the blue sky above;

That doubt and trouble, fear and pain,
And anguish, — these are shadows vain;
That death itself shall not remain;

That weary deserts we may tread,
Dreary perplexities may thread,
Through dark ways underground be led;

Yet we, on divers shores now cast,
Shall meet, when this dark storm is past,
Safe in our Father's home at last.

And, ere thou leave him, say thou this,
Yet one thing more: they only miss
The speedy winning of that bliss, —

Who will not count it true, that love,
Blessing, *not* cursing, rules above;
And that in this we live and move.

And one thing further: let him know,
That, to believe these things are so,
This firm faith never to forego

In spite of all that seems at strife
With blessing — all with cursing rife,
That this is blessing, this is life."

V.

THE FOLLY OF SOLOMON.

ECCLES. i. 2: "All is vanity."

ALMOST three thousand years ago, a little child was born to David, King of Israel, whose advent was felt to be such a blessing, that he was called Solomon, or "Peace." He was carefully reared, as befitted the future ruler of the nation; had natural gifts of surpassing excellence; was diligent in their improvement; and, so far as we can now ascertain, was the foremost scholar in the land at that time. The nation of which he was destined to be the ruler was then touching the summit of its greatness; and this prince became to Jewry what Alexander, at a later day, was to Greece, and Augustus to Rome. He came to the throne in due time, and the people shouted, "God save the king!" His public life opened beautifully and well. He made wise treaties as a king, and wonderful decisions as a judge. He developed commerce, manufactures, literature, and art; edited, and partly wrote, one book which, in those early days got unquestioned canonization, and, in a measure deserved it.

He was also the founder and finisher of the first temple on Zion, and offered the first prayer at its consecration. That prayer has come down to us: it reveals a sincere and religious nature. Then he was a great student, philosopher, musician, and landscape gardener; created a beautiful home, and married a wife more of his free choice than commonly falls to the lot of kings. In a word, one thinks he was about all a man can be, and gathered all a man can get, in this world, to make him content and happy. Then, when he had done, he wrote a sermon, in which he tried to tell what it was all worth. That sermon is the Book of Ecclesiastes, and its burden is the text I have read you. And I want to give you the kernel of the discourse, in a few representative sentences, selected from the whole book.

The preacher begins by declaring, that all the things that happen are an endless repetition. The sun rises and sets; the wind veers round and round; the waters are lifted out of the sea, and poured in again. Man is a part of this endless round; race after race sweeps on, all alike and all alike forgotten; so that which has been shall be, and there is no new thing under the sun. "I have tried it," cries the preacher. "I was a king, and what can any man do more than a king? I tell you it is vanity; and you cannot make the crooked straight, or number what is wanting. Things are set fast as they are, and so they will stay; and he that increases knowledge increases sorrow. I tried pleasure, planted gardens, opened fountains, indulged in wine and mirth and music. I know exactly what these can do for a man; and there is no profit in them. I found them vanity; so I hated all my labor that I had done under the sun. Then I dipped into fatalism. I said, 'What is to be will be; there is a time for every thing under the sun,—a time to be born, and a time to die; a time to weep, and a time to laugh; a time to love, and a time to hate; a time to get, and a time to lose; a time to pull down, and a time to build up.' And, when the time comes, the man must do his work; but then this is van ity : for, if a man act so blindly, what is he more than a beast? There *is* no pre-eminence; fate is master of both; all spring from the dust, all go to the dust; all is vanity. Then I tried man. But I saw the oppressed, and they had no comforter; and the oppressor, and he had no comfort. So I praised the dead more than the living, and that which never knew life more than they both. For I saw that every man was for himself; and, though he had neither child nor brother, he never said, ' Why do I starve my life for gain ? ' All is vanity. What is a wise man more than a fool ? Who can tell a man what is good, when all his days are as a shadow ? Sorrow is better than laughter; the end is better than the beginning. A just man perishes by his own justice, while a wicked man prolongs his life in his wickedness. Nay, come to that, there is no just man on this earth. I have studied the thing out: there is not one man in a thousand upright, and not one woman in the world. Don't be righteous overmuch or wicked overmuch. I see the wicked get the reward of the good, and the good the reward of the wicked. A man has no better thing under the sun than to eat and drink and be merry; for there is no certainty. The dead know not any thing. There is no wisdom or knowledge or device in the grave whither we all hasten. And the race is not to the swift, or the battle to the strong; or bread to the wise, or fame to the skilful. Servants ride on horses; princes trudge on foot. You cannot alter the thing: it is so, and so it will be. If you dig a pit, you will fall into it; if you move a hedge, a serpent will bite you; if you take down a wall, the stones will bruise you; if you listen, you will hear your servant curse you. Money will buy any thing. All is vanity. Childhood and youth is vanity; old age is vanity. Vanity of vanities, all is vanity."

This, my friends, is the substance of this great man's last estimate of life. You read it, and, as you read, you watch the writer trying to fight down the black shadows as they rise. Here and there, too, all through his sermon, he will say a noble thing on the right side; as if the old power of piety was strong enough yet to burn through, and force its way to the parchment. But, when the best is said and done, the result is a belief in a God who exacts more than he gives, and punishes more readily than he blesses. He seems sometimes to think, if a man will take good care, there may be some small chance of content for him. Still he is all the while afraid he may say too much on that side, and is ready at every turn to let you see the death's head within the folds of his vesture. Here and there a pleasant note is just sounded, and you say, "Now we are to have a bit of gospel, or a song of thanksgiving." But the gospel is never heard; the song is never sung. The heavy, solemn chord beats along steadily to the last; and the burden is always, "All is vanity."

And so it is that this woful estimate of life has made this book by far the most difficult to understand in the whole range of the Scriptures. Down to the time of Jerome, there were pious Jews not a few who held that it had better be destroyed. It has taxed the ingenuity of commentators, who have differed over it as only commentators can. For the book has that about it that will be heard. The writer was, in such wisdom as it was, the wisest man of his era. He had matchless opportunities of knowing what the life really is he condemns so sternly. He speaks to you with a most evident, sad, painful good faith, that makes you feel sure he means every word he says. And then the book is set fast among our Sacred Scriptures. The statements in it are as positive as any other. Solomon is as clear when he says, "Man has no pre-eminence over a beast," as John is when he says, "Beloved, now are we the sons of God." So it comes to pass, that, if you take this book as it stands, and undertake to believe it, the result is very sad. It chills all piety, paralyzes all effort, hushes all prayer. If there is grief in wisdom, had I not better be a fool? If all labor is vanity, and a man is no better than a beast, and rewards and punishments are a dire confusion, and childhood and youth and old age is vanity, and to die is better than to live, because there is nothing worth living or dying for, — then this is —

"A life of nothings, nothing worth, —
From that first nothing ere our birth
To the last nothing under earth."

It cannot be denied, again, that the book is but the vocal utterance of many a silent sermon in many a lonely heart. It was this, no doubt, that made it the text-book of Voltaire and the bosom-friend of Frederick the Great. Its monotones of despair are echoed out of a thousand experiences. When a friend wished a great English statesman a happy new year, "Happy!" he said; "it had need be happier than the last, for in that I never knew one happy day." When an English lawyer, whose life had seemed to be one long range of success, mounted the last step in his profession, he wrote, "In a few weeks I shall retire to dear Encombe, as a short resting-place between vexation and the grave." When one said to the great Rothschild, "You must be a happy man," he replied, "I sleep with pistols under my pillow." The most brilliant man of the world in the last century said, "I have enjoyed all the pleasures of life, and I do not regret their loss; I have been behind the scenes, and seen the coarse pulleys and ropes and tallow-candles." And the most brilliant poet of the last generation said, "The lapse of ages changes all but man, who ever has been, and will be, an unlucky rascal. And one of the finest promise, dying in his first prime, left us this estimate, that —

> "All this passing scene
> Is a peevish April day;
> A little sun, a little rain,
> And then death sweeps along the plain,
> And all things fade away."

Nay, may I not leave these dead, and come to the living to find a legion of men in Europe and America, ready to indorse this as their own estimate of life, — men who feel that life is weary, and fear that death is but a dead, blank wall; who have come to consider the forces of life and nature things that grind on so immutably as to leave them no heart to pray; who see those whose life is a shame before heaven rosy and happy, and threescore and ten; while others, whose life had begun to be a very fountain of inspiration and blessing, are cut off in their prime? And so they cry, "How can there be a Divine Providence?" and ponder over life, and pare down faith to their contracting and contracted hope, until a living faith in God dies out of their heart; and then they lose a real faith in any thing, as Solomon did. For I tell you, that, as the outer life takes its deepest meaning from the soul, the inner life takes its deepest meaning from God; and, when that goes, all goes. When a man ceases to believe in God, he is in instant danger of ceasing to believe in any thing worth the name of belief. In open-eyed loyalty and trust, and trustful men and things, all these vanish, and he can see only —

> "Good statesmen, who bring ruin on a state;
> Good patriots, who for a theory risk a cause;
> Good priests, who bring all good to jeopardy;
> Good Christians, who sit still in easy-chairs,
> And damn the general world for standing up."

Now, then, for all this, I have but one answer. *I cannot believe it.* In the deepest meaning of the truth and the life, this assertion that all is vanity is utterly untrue. It is no matter to me that the man who wrote it is sometimes called "the wisest man;" that he was in deadly earnest about it; that it was his own woful experience; and, if you could add to this, that an angel had come from heaven to re-affirm it. All this is gossamer before the conviction of every wholesome and healthy mind, that in this universe there is an infinitely different meaning. God never meant life to be vanity; and life is not vanity. I care not that Solomon look at me out of his great sad eyes, and say so, while his heart breaks; and that Dundas and Eldon and Byron and Kirke White range with him. I will not, you will not, and millions beside in the world and out of it will not, testify that all is vanity.

And that we are right and all such men wrong can be proven, I think, outside our own experience, on several different counts. For, first of all, this Solomon is not the right man to testify. When he said this of life, he was in no condition to tell the truth about it, and he did *not* tell the truth. Universal testimony makes this sermon the fruit of his old age. There is a dim tradition, that the book was found in fragments after his death, edited, and the last six verses added, — and they are the best in the book, — by another hand. If this book was the work of Solomon's old age, the fact of itself supplies the first reason why we have such a sermon; for the man who wrote this sermon, and the youth who offered that noble prayer at the dedication of the temple, are not the same men. The young king knelt down in the bloom of his youth, when the fountains of life were pure and clean; when through and through his soul great floods of power and grace rose to springtide every day; when the processions of nature and providence, the numbers of the poet, the wisdom of the sage, the labors of the reformer, and the sacrifices of the patriot, were steeped for him in their rarest beauty, endowed with their loftiest meaning, and filled with their uttermost power. But that old king in the palace, writing his sermon, is weary and worn; and, worst of all, the clear fountains of his nature are changed to puddles; the fresh, strong life has been squandered away; the delicate, divine perception blunted, clogged, and at last smothered to death. You know how, in his later life, this man fell from his great estate; and, to gratify his passion and pride, outraged the most sacred ordinances, and neglected the most sacred duties, that can cluster round any life. His biographer compresses the whole sad story into one chapter; but, if you will read that, you can see how fearfully he had fallen, — how haggard vices had supplanted fair virtues, and successful rebellion taken the place of "God save the king." It is when he sits in that splendid, cheerless home; when the sceptre totters in his palsied hand, and the bloom of purity and grace has gone out of him; when his sin has made him blind to the blessing of books and nature and home and God, and his bad life has magnetized bad men toward him, and driven good men away; and his relation to woman is of such a nature as to drive him from the presence of such pure and noble women as, thank God, never fail out of the world, and never will; satirists and Solomons to the contrary, notwithstanding; it is when he has spent all this substance in riotous living, and reduced himself to an utter destitution of the heart and soul, — that he will write his final estimate of God, nature, life, death, books, and men and women. Can we wonder that such a man should write " all is vanity," when he had come to be the vanity he wrote?

But, then, I ask you, was this the time to make the estimate, when the man was all dissonant to the touch of the divine finger; or was that the time when every faculty was chorded and attuned, and he stood in harmony with life, and the experience on which his estimate was founded was the sweet music that came out of the communion of his soul with God? Believe me, we cannot form the true estimate when the life is ruined. What he said when he was his best self, before his ruin, was true; and the estimate he made, when he was a lower man, was as much out of true as the man was.

Then there was an error in this man's *method* of testing life, that I suspect to be at the root of much of the weariness that is still felt; and that is, the man does not seem to have tried to be happy, in making others happy, in bringing one gleam more of gladness, or one pulse more of life, into any soul save his own. In the sad days recorded here, nature, books, men, women, were worth to him just what they could do for him. When he gave up being good, and took to being wise, he never more drank at that fountain which is the source of all true blessedness, but made his wisdom a cistern; and, lo! it was cracked and fissured in every direction. He gave up the present sense of God in the soul; the high uses of worship; the inspiration hidden in great books; the deep blessedness of being father, husband, friend, teacher, patriot, and reformer; buried himself in his harem; turned a deaf ear to all the pleadings of his better angel; and, when he had come to this, who can wonder that all was vanity?

But now I must state the reason, that to me is greatest of all, why I know all is *not* vanity. A thousand years after this sad sermon was written, there was born of the same great line another little child. He had no royal training, no waiting sceptre, no kingly palace, but the ten der nurture of a noble mother, and, from the first, a wonderful nearness to God, — and that was all. He grew up in a country town that had become a proverb of worthlessness. The neighbors, when he is a man, cannot remember that he ever learned his letters. He stood at the carpenter's bench, working for his bread, until he was perhaps thirty years old; and then it was given to him to preach another sermon, and make another estimate. He was endowed with a power to see into the nature of this world and its life, such as never fell to the lot of another on the earth. The good he knew, and the bad he knew, as I suppose it was never known before. The human heart was laid bare before him down to its deepest recesses. None ever felt, as he did, the curse of sin, or had such a perfect loyalty and love for holiness. Nature, Providence, Heaven, and Hell were actual presences, solid certainties to his deep, true sight. He came out of the carpenter's shop; and when he had pondered over this solemn question of life in the solitudes beyond Jordan, it was laid, I say, upon him, as it had been laid on his fore-elder long before, to preach on the mighty theme. That sermon also has come down to us. It was as sure to do that, as the sun was that shone when he was preaching it; and to me the difference between the two sermons bridges the whole distance between the two great estimates of life, taught on this side by the Saviour, and on that by Solomon.

Listen while I try the ring of a few sentences from each of them. "Vanity of vanities, all is vanity," cries the first preacher. "Blessed are the poor, blessed are the mourners, blessed are the quiet, blessed are the hungry for the right, blessed are the giving and forgiving, blessed are the pure-hearted, blessed are the peace-makers, and blessed are the sufferers for the right," cries the second. "Be not righteous overmuch," cries the first. "Be ye perfect, even as your Father in heaven is perfect," cries the second. "That which befalleth a beast, befalleth a man," cries the first. "The very hairs of your head are numbered," cries the second. "There is no knowledge nor wisdom nor device in the grave," cries the first. "I go to prepare a place for you; and I will come again, and take you to myself, that where I am, there ye may be also," cries the second.

This last preacher tested life also. Whatever can be done to prove all is vanity, was done to him. Giving out blessing, getting back cursing. Surely, if ever man would write "Vanity of vanities" over life, this was the man to do it; if ever one has made life unspeakably noble and good through a perfect belief in it, it was this man. The madman crouching among the tombs, the lost woman on the street, the seaman on the wharf, and the beggar full of sores, — all stood in the first glory of a celestial life, as he saw them, the lily on the green sward, the bird on the spray, and the child in the gutter, claimed in his heart kinship with the cherubim and seraphim up in heaven. God was to him the Father. The future life was more of a reality than the present. He saw *resurgam* written over every grave, and could see past sorrow and pain, the perfect end, and say, "Of all that my Father has given me, I have lost nothing: he will raise it up at the last day."

Now, I look out at life with you, and we can no more solve some of its problems than could this sad-hearted king, because we have in our own lives some darkness or trouble like that which he felt.

There are moments in our experience when fate seems to block out prayer, when the awful steadfastness of nature comes in like a dead wall against providence, and the vision is clouded, and the heart is faint. It is because we have the black drop in our veins that we may ponder the great problems of life, sometimes until our hearts break, and yet be no nearer their solution, — what is either microscope or telescope to a blind man. But as I grieve over these things, and come no nearer, I hear this strong voice of a greater than Solomon, crying, " Come unto me, all ye that labor and are heavy laden, and I will give you rest." Then, if I cannot see heaven of myself, let me look at it through his eyes. If earth grows empty and worthless to me, let me believe in what it was to him, and be sure that he is the Way the Truth and the Life; so, holding fast by faith in him, I may come at last to a faith in earth and heaven and life and the life to come, and all that is most indispensable to the soul. For so it is, that he is the Mediator between God and man; helps my unbelief; ever liveth to make intercession for me; that he is still eyes to the blind, and feet to the lame; that he preaches deliverance to the captives, and the opening of prison doors to them that are bound. If I cannot pray because I see no reason, then that bended figure on Olivet is my reason. If I cannot distinguish between fate and providence, let me rejoice that he can, and that my blindness can make no difference to his blessing. So, under *this* Captain of my salvation, I shall be more than conqueror; and, while the mournful outcry is rising about me, "Vanity of vanities, all is vanity," in my heart shall be the confidence that all things work together for good.

> "And nothing walks with aimless feet,
> And not one life shall be destroyed,
> Or cast as rubbish to the void,
> When God has made the pile complete."

VI.

FAITH.

HEB. xi. 1: "Faith . . . the evidence of things not seen."

WHEN the author of the Epistle to the Hebrews has made this masterly definition of a true faith, he instantly proceeds to make the thing clear by illustration. He says, among other things, a man once started out from the old home, to settle in a new country. He did not know his destination, only his direction. Somewhere west by south lay the land he was to own; and so west by south he went. He was possessed by two great ideas: one was to make a new home; the other, to fill that home with children, and so become the founder of a family. He came to the land at last, and was sure about its being the right place, because the same thing occurred to assure him of it that had first led him to seek it. The voice in his soul, he had learned to know as the voice of God, told him so.

But time went on. He lived to be an old man before he had one legitimate son ; and died before that son — then getting into years, and very shiftless — had children born to him. And all the land he could call his own, when the end came, was a field he had bought years before, as a cemetery for his dead. This was what his life-long faith had brought him as a pledge that it was a faith and not a fancy, — a shiftless, childless son, and a graveyard. This man, says the writer, was your ancestor; and he lived and died as fully satisfied that every thing would come out right, as if he had seen the land in your possession these fifteen centuries, and seen you swarming as the stars in the sky for multitude.

Then he tells of another, — a man educated, refined, intellectual, and directly in the way of becoming almost any thing he could wish to be, in one of the foremost nations on the earth. In the country, at that time, there was an alien race, — ignorant, oppressed, and so hateful to those who oppressed them, that they never sat down together at the same table. In the outset of his career, that young man turned his back on all his bright prospects, took sides with the despised and hated brickmakers,— for that was what they had come to; gave up the society of cultivated men, the occupations of the scholar and gentleman, and the use that must have become a second nature; went over and stood beside the poor multitude ; identified himself with them ; went to work as a shepherd, until the time should come to emancipate them from their thraldom; pondered the thing over in the grassy solitudes of Midian ; and then, when he had got so full of it that he could be quiet no longer, went up to court, bearded the king in his palace, and demanded their freedom. That man, says this writer, was your lawgiver; and he did this because he had the faith in the future which your ancestor had. Here, he said, is the making of a nation, and I am to make it. Across the desert is the land they are to occupy; and I am to lead them to it. Forty years after, he was at the end of his career. All that time he had striven for the fulfilment of his purpose, had endured every thing and done every thing, with this faith in his heart, — that there was sure to be success at the end.

Then, when they were quite ready to go in and

take the land, the man knew that for him all was over; that the deep longing of eighty years was not to be given him; he could never stand on the land he had made every sacrifice to reach. But there was a mountain-top that commanded the country: he would go there, and take one great look at it. He went up; it lay glancing in the sun, as Switzerland lies about the feet of the Rhigi; and, with the light of it in his eyes, he died. God's angel kissed him, and he slept. But, as he looked his last, he no more doubted that the nation for which, fourscore years before, he had pawned his position, prospects, likings, and life, would live on that land, and be in some way what he had wrought for, than if he had seen it already dotted with their towers and towns. And this was his motive-power, " Faith . . . the evidence of things not seen."

What a mighty thing as a motive-power, then, this faith must be! If a man is possessed by it, that something can be done; in some sure sense, it is done already, and only waits its time to come into visible existence in the best way it can. Just as one of those noble groups John Rogers fashions for us is done the moment the conception of it has struck his heart with a pang of delight, though he may not have so much as the lump of clay for his beginning; while I might stand with the clay in my hand to doomsday, and not make what he does, because I could not have the "Faith . . . the evidence of things not seen."

Indeed this is the sense I would put on that strange saying of Jesus,—"If ye have faith to say to that mountain, 'Be thou removed and cast into the sea,' it shall be done,"—that what he wants to impress on us is not so much the mountain riven out of its deep fastnesses on the earth, as the faith abiding in its deeper fastnesses in the heart. "If ye have faith, it shall be done," I conceive to be the true reading, as the true teaching is, What cannot be done, cannot be of faith. There can be no real faith in the soul toward the impossible; but make sure that faith is there, and then you can form no conception of the surprises of power hidden in the heart of it.

And, trying to make this thing clear to you, I know of no better way to begin, than by saying, that faith is never that airy nothing which often usurps its place, and for which I can find no better name than fancy,—a feeling without fitness, an anticipation without an antecedent, an effect without a cause, a cipher without a unit.

In the dawn of his life, a lad will say, "I am going to be a merchant prince, or a metropolitan preacher." It is a noble purpose, if it can sink into his soul, deepen and enrich his nature, and so become the ladder by which he will rise into the heaven of his hope. But if to be what he dreams he merely dreams, cribs his lessons, shirks his duties, and conducts himself generally like a loafer,— what he may call a faith is merely a very foolish fancy, founded on nothing, and sure to end in nothing but disappointment.

Or he may prepare a plan of his life at thirty, on the theory that this world, with all its treasures, is a sort of big sweet orange he can suck with an endless gusto, and then give Lazarus the skin; and, whether he has money already or has to make it, is determined to have a good time, because he believes that was what orange and appetite are made for. Now, is that a faith in the world and life? No: it is a fancy that will leave his orange at last as savorless as a potato-rind, or as bitter as soot; and set him some day longing to get the cup of cold water out of the hand of the meanest man he ever left to rot, if he could only hope to get with it the power that man has to quench his thirst. Or he will make ready for the life to come, by saying prayers, going through motions, making professions, shirking responsibilities, worrying down doubts, and pampering a minister. And he will call that faith. Is it faith? It is the merest fancy, the play of the imagination, to the hurt of the man, hurtful every time, and leading to tragical ends, whether in the daydream of the idle boy or the awful soliloquies of Hamlet.

Fancies are never, at our peril, to be mistaken for faith. They may feel just as good, and in some wild way they are as good, to the maniac strutting in his crown of straw, as to the king on his throne. It is because they have no intimate and inevitable relation to the set and nature and law and life of things. And so they can never be the evidence of *things* not seen. A mere fancy, to a pure faith, is as the "Arabian Nights" to the Sermon on the Mount.

Then faith is not something standing clean at the other extreme from fancy, for which there is no better name than fatalism, — a condition numbers are continually drifting into, who, from their very earnestness, are in no danger of being sucked into the whirlpools of fancy; men who glance at the world and life through the nightglass of Mr. Buckle; who look backward and there is eternity, and forward and there is eternity; and feel all about them, and conclude that they are in the grasp of a power beside which what they can do to help themselves is about what a chip can do on the curve at Niagara.

And yet their nature may be far too bright and wholesome to permit them to feel, that the drift of things is not on the whole for good. They will be ready even to admit that "our souls are organ-pipes of diverse stop and various pitch, each with its proper note thrilling beneath the self-same touch of God." But, when a hard pinch comes, they smoke their pipe, and refer it to Allah, or cover their face and refer it to Allah; but never fight it out, inch by inch, with all their heart and soul, in the sure faith that things will be very much after all what they make them,— that the Father worketh hitherto, and they work. And these two things — the fancy that things will come to pass because we dream them, and the fatalism that they will come to pass because we cannot avoid them — are never to be mistaken for faith.

It is true that there is both a fancy and a fatalism that is perfectly sound and good, — the fancy that clothes the future to an earnest lad with a sure hope; that keeps the world fresh and fair, as in natures like that of Leigh Hunt, when to most men it has become arid as desert dust; — the bloom and poetry, thank God, by which men are converted, and become as little children. And there is a fatalism that touches the very centre of the circle of faith, — which Paul always had in his soul. When sounding out some mighty affirmation of the sovereignty of God, he would go right on, with a more perfect and trusting devotion to work in the line of it. Fancy and fatalism, are the strong handmaidens of faith: happy is the man whose faith they serve.

But what, then, is faith? Can that be made clear? I think it can; and, to do it, I will go back to the illustrations I cited at the start; very noble and good, as I doubt not you are aware, when they are divested of the unreal wonders the worship of the ages has gathered about them.

A young man feels in his heart the conviction, that there in the future is waiting for him a great destiny. Yet that destiny depends on his courage, and that courage on his constancy; and it is only when each has opened into the other, that the three become that evidence of things not seen, on which he can die with his soul satisfied, — though all the land he had to show for the one promise was a graveyard; and all the line for the other, a childless son. Another feels a conviction, that here at his hand is a great work to do, — a nation to create out of a degraded mob, and to settle in a land where it can carry out his ideas and its own destiny. But the conviction can be nothing without courage; and courage, a mere rushing into the jaws of destruction, without constancy. Only when forty years had gone, and the steady soul had fought its fight, did conviction, courage, and constancy ripen into the full certainty which shone in the eyes of the dying statesman, as he stood on Nebo, and death was swallowed up in victory. And yet it is clear, that, while courage and constancy in these men was essential to their faith, faith again was essential to their courage and constancy. These were the meat and drink on which the faith depended; but the faith was the life for which the meat and drink were made. A dim, indefinable consciousness at first it was, that something was waiting in that direction, a treasure hid in that field somewhere, to be their own if they durst but sell all they had, and buy the field. Then, as bit by bit they paid the price in the pure gold of some new responsibility or sacrifice, the clear certainty took the place of the dim intimation, and faith became the evidence of things not seen.

This is the way a true faith always comes. Conversing once with a most faithful woman, I found that the way she came to be what she is lay at first along a dark path, in which she had to take one little timid step at a time. But, as she went on, she found all the more reason to take another and another, until God led her by a way she knew not, and brought her into a large place. Yet it was a long while before any step did not make the most painful drafts on both her courage and constancy. And so the whole drift of what man has done for man and God is the story of such a leading, — first a consciousness that the thing must be done, then a spark of courage to try and do it; then a constancy that endures to the end; and then, whatever the end may be, — the prison or the palace, it is all the same, — the soul has the evidence of things not seen, and goes singing into her rest.

Now, then, a faith like this must be a prime thing in your life and mine, or we shall make a dead failure of it; and it must be rooted in us, as it was in these old-time men, in a sure conviction of some divine intention to be wrought out by our living.

There is a trick of humility, in some men, I cannot believe to be good. It is that which makes them so very humble, that they cannot try to do a thing worth the notice of earth or heaven. Believe me, that is not a possession, but a destitution. It is not because I have humility when I feel like that, but because I want faith. I can see nothing noble in myself, because I have not the evidence of things *not* seen. Well may any man be humble, in a fair, manly, and manful humility; but, I tell you, the humility that will lead me to believe myself a nobody, a cipher, a stick, in this great destiny-laden world and time, is no better than a delusion and a snare. What I can do with my single arm may be mean enough; but that is not the question. The thing to consider is, What can I do with God to help me? And the difference of the one and the other way is just the difference between a man trying to push a train of cars up grade by his single, puny strength, and the same man on a locomotive, with the steam up, moving the whole mass by a turn of the wrist. The man at the rear of the train can do nothing: how should he? But give him the lever, and the faith which is the evidence of things not seen, and all things are possible; because then, in what his hand finds to do, there is hidden a treasure of power unspeakably greater than his own. The fire of an old world before Adam, the life-long energy and inspiration of Watt and Stephenson, the ponderous strokes of the Nasmyth hammer, and the labors of a thousand men, all lock into his hand the moment it touches that lever

Now, then, we want to make sure of three things, then we shall know that this faith is our own: 1. That God is at work without me, — that is, the divine energy, — as fresh and full before I came, as the sea is before the minnow comes; 2. That he is at work through me, — that is, the divine intention, — as certainly present in my life as it was in the life of Moses; and, 3. That what we do together is as sure to be a success as that we are striving to make it one. There may be more in the graveyard than there is in the home. In the moment toward which I have striven forty years with a tireless, passionate, hungry energy, my expectation may be cut off, while my eye is as bright and my step as firm as ever. It is no matter. The energy is as full, the intention as direct, and the accomplishment as sure, as though God had already made the pile complete. And when, with the conviction that I can do a worthy thing, and the courage to try and the constancy to keep on, I can cast myself, as Paul did, and Moses and Abraham, into the arms of a perfect assurance of this energy, intention, and accomplishment of the Eternal, — feel, in every fibre of my nature, that in Him

I live and move and have my being,—I shall not fear, though the earth be removed, because—

> "A faith like this for ever doth impart
> Authentic tidings of invisible things;
> Of ebb and flow, and ever-during power,
> And central peace, subsisting at the heart
> Of endless agitation."

Let the lad, in this spirit, dream of his great place, then, and strike for it with all his might; and the man, in the thick of this world's work, take heart as these old Hebrews did, and be sure that to do what honest thing he has to do, with courage and constancy as long as he lives, is not only the way to heaven hereafter, but the way to make heaven a solid and shining reality now. Hume said the teaching of ethics in England improved the manufacture of broadcloth. I doubt not that the broadcloth re-acted again on the ethics, because all things work together for good to them that love God.

But one word waits now to be said. There, on the summit of all great doing, stands one whose life is the light of men; because, beyond all men, there came into his heart this conviction, that he had a great destiny, and the courage to live for it, and the constancy to hold on to it, together ogies ?. A child on tiptoe with its eyes wide open, expecting, because an intimation has come, that presently there will be something to see or receive; the nestling in its cradle, waiting for its sure morsel. That was the way in which our first fathers tried to express their idea of what hope is, and what it can do. They said, "As a child opens its eyes, and a young bird its mouth, so is true hope in the soul of a man," — expectation and intimation together, certainty reaching through change, the flutter of a fledgling's heart, welded fast to immutable law.

These meanings to me, again, are the delicate dividing line between Faith and Hope. They are twin sisters, and hardly to be known apart; both as beautiful as they can be, and alike beautiful, and very often indeed mistaken each for the other. Yet this need never be; because between them there is this clear difference, that while Hope expects, Faith inspects; while Hope is like Mary, looking *up*-ward, Faith is like Martha, looking *at*-ward; while the light in the eyes of Hope is high, the light in the eyes of Faith is strong; while Hope trembles in expectation, Faith is quiet in possession. Hope leaps out toward what will be;

Faith holds on to what is; Hope idealizes, Faith realizes; Faith sees, Hope foresees.

And so it comes, that, in what we call religion, faith is conservative, while hope is progressive. And the most hopeful men are always drawn into the new movements of their age, and are faithful to them, so long as they can remember Goethe's exhortation, to be true to the dream of their youth. For progression is up stream, while conservatism is on stream. And so, if a man gets afraid, as Luther did, or tired with Erasmus, there is no need that he should get out of the boat, or pull back : all he need do is just leave go of the stroke-oar, and the thing will go back of itself fast enough. It is so that not a few who were progressive men at twenty-five are conservative men at fifty-five ; yet are not aware that they have done a thing to make themselves conservative. It is so that some Unitarians are far less liberal than some Orthodox, who were once a long way behind them ; not that they ever pulled back, but they did not pull forward, while the Orthodox did. Now they are away down below ; and only do not go lower, because they have drifted into the still waters in which it is a matter of the most absolute indifference which way they may be heading. In their youth, their watchword was, " Be sure you are right, and then, — go ahead;" in their age it is, " Be sure you are right, and then, — hold on." The trouble with such men is, that, while they hold on to the faith, they have let go of the hope of their religion. And so they inspect, but they do not expect; they believe in what has come, but not in what is coming. So they expire after they have ceased to inspire; they die, but they do *not* make many live.

You get a grand lesson on this matter, as you go from the mouth to the springs of the Rhine. Passing through the fog and mist of Holland, as through a stagnant, grassy sea, you stretch upward, league after league; and, as you go, the country gradually changes. The air grows clearer, the prospect finer; every thing that can stir the soul begins to reach down toward you, and touch you with its glory. But the higher you go, the harder is your going; only the deepening beauty never fails you. So at last you come into Switzerland, where the blue heavens bend over you with their infinite, tender light; and the mountains stand about you, in their white robes, glorious as the gates of heaven, with green valleys nestling between, that, but for sorrow and sin, are beautiful as Paradise. And all about you is a vaster vision, and within you an intenser inspiration than can ever be felt on the foggy flats below.

It is *the* difference between faith alone, and faith and hope together. A man may be afloat on this river of the water of life, down on the stagnant flats of Romanism; or he may pull up to the outposts of the mountains, and, looking up and down, may say, "That is enough for me; now I will go no further." Or he may look up, and see still, blue, misty distances, hinting of a glory his eye has not seen or his heart conceived; and then go on again, full of hope, until the uttermost glory receives him into its heart. I do not claim this great place, for my *ism* or any other. When the thing is done, it is generally done by a man who has broken away from the *isms;* some uplooking, steady, hopeful soul, that, —

"Rowing hard against the stream,
Sees distant gates of Eden gleam,
And doth not dream it is a dream."

For it must be true, as God is true, that the uttermost. is the holiest truth ; and, not until a man shall win his way to the very steps of the great white throne, can he at his peril inspect and cease to expect, — be content with possession, and not discontent with desire, — have such an absolute faith in any revelation, as to have no hope of a higher and better.

This brings me, then, to the consideration of hope itself as a positive matter. And, in discussing this, I cannot do better than begin with the figure the apostle has caught, and ask you to notice the striking contrast it presents to many of our common ideas of what hope is, and what it can do.

Hope, you say. Why, that is the most intangible thing a man can entertain. It is the mere poetry of life, — the play of summer lightning on the night, the meteor shower across heaven, the sheen of the aurora in winter. "Hope," says Owen Feltham, "is the bladder a man will take wherewith to learn to swim; then he goes beyond return, and is lost." And Lee, —

"Hope is the fawning traitor of the mind,
Which, while it cozens with a colored friendship,
Robs us of our best virtue, — resolution."

Now, what says Paul? He has a picture in his

eye of a Roman soldier, with bronze shoes, brazen greaves, breastplate, sword, shield; a quick eye, strong hand, steady foot, and a legion shoulder to shoulder, as cool in the thick of the battle as if it was on dress-parade. But that is because there is one thing more, wanting, which the man's hand and foot and eye and sword and shield would all come short of his need, when he has to hold his own against the battle-axe of the barbarian, — and that is the solid, shining helmet. So the apostle makes our life a battle, and every man a soldier, and it is not enough that the heart be protected by the shield of faith, — the head must be guarded also by the helmet of hope: the one is as indispensable as the other.

And a brief glance at the life about us will soon convince you that the man is right. Whether we dip into our own experience, or watch that of other men, we shall still conclude, with wise old Samuel Johnson, that our powers owe very much of their energy to our hope; and whatever enlarges hope exalts courage; and, where there is no hope, there is no endeavor.

Here is Cyrus Field conceiving the idea of binding the Atlantic with a cord, — of making that awful crystal dome a whispering gallery between two worlds, — of fulfilling afresh, in these last times, the old prophecy, that "as the lightning cometh out of the east, and shineth even unto the west, so shall also the coming of the Son of man be." In carrying out his idea, the man has two servants to help him, — the faith that it can be done, and the hope that he shall do it. With these aids he goes to work. Faith steadies him; hope inspires him. Faith works; hope flies. Faith deliberates; hope anticipates. Faith lets the cable go, and it breaks, and is lost. "Nay, not lost," cries hope, and fishes it up again. If hope had struck work in Cyrus Field, and faith alone had remained, we should not this day have had this *nexus* formed of his manhood, by which the world will be born again to a new life. But there, through the long day, the noble sisters stood, — faith in Ireland, hope in Newfoundland; faith in the Old World, hope in the New. Faith threw the cord, hope caught it. And " I saw a great angel stand with one foot on the sea, and another on the land; and he sware by Him that liveth, that *time shall be no more.*"

Here is Garibaldi conceiving the idea of a new Italy. He has faith and hope. Austria, Naples, and Rome are against him. But no man knows, or can know, what faith and hope together can do in a man of the pattern of Garibaldi. What they have done for Italy will go ringing down the ages. They have " subdued kingdoms, wrought righteousness, escaped the edge of the sword, turned to flight the armies of the aliens. Women have received their dead to life again; others were tortured, not accepting deliverance, that they might obtain the better resurrection." And in these very days they are singing a song, as we sang " John Brown's body " and the " Battle-cry of Freedom;" and its burden is their hope that Italy will be free. And if that man shall still keep his hands clasped in the hands of these sisters, this good work will never cease, until Italy shall rise clean out of the dust, and the old mistress of the world begin a new career; in which her greatness will be counted, as all true greatness is counted, by the worth and weight of the service she can render to the race.

Very curiously, if you will again, you can see the power of faith without hope illustrated in

China. There you see a nation, beside which in numbers we are only a handful, that has had for ages as much faith and as little hope as ever entered into any civilization. When our ancestors were savages, they had advanced about where they are now. Things we consider the morning stars of our new life were known to them centuries before we invented them! And who shall say what China might not have been to-day, had she marched on under the banner of a boundless hope? But she had faith without hope. She said, " My learning, literature, science, art, religion are all as good as they can be. If any man shall add unto these things, I will add unto him plagues; and, if any man shall take away from these things, I will take away his part out of the book of life." It is in vain that Raphael has painted, and Angelo builded; and that holy men, from of old, have written as they were inspired by the Holy Ghost. What is St. Peter's to the great Pagoda, or the Immaculate Conception to the gilded Joss, or the Evangels to Confucius, or the Monitor to the royal junk, or any other thing we can show, to the glory of the children of the Sun? So the vast empire sits still on the stagnant waters of conservatism, with faith, without hope; inspecting for ever, expecting no more, and with Russia creeping stealthily toward a point where she can get a fair sight at her heart. Then some day, there will be a shot, and a great dead carcass, to which the Lion of England will gather with the Northern Bear; and on which the Eagle of America will swoop down swiftly, screaming defiance as she flies at the Eagle of France. But who shall say, that China, with the noble qualities no doubt she has, might not have had a peerless place in the world, had she held herself hopeful and expectant, continually, toward every new idea and discovery,—had she taken for a helmet the hope of salvation?

And, altogether, this fact of hope and its influence has some important applications. First, in the application of hope to religion, to the deepest and highest things of which we have any knowledge, it is entirely essential to remember, that, when this man tells his friends to take for a helmet the hope of salvation, he meant the hope he himself was rushing through the world to proclaim, with such an abandon of enthusiasm, as to make a cool, dispassionate Roman call him a lunatic.

So that the first thing really in the exhortation is the hopefulness of the exhorter. The man had, for that old time, just what Cyrus Field had on the Stock Exchange in London, — the splendid contagion of a great hope, as reasonable to him as the coldest mathematical demonstration, while yet it might seem to the mathematician a mere wild dream. And this is always the first thing, the greater thing than faith, — the power that sings what faith can only say, the perfect music to the noble word.

In the England of John Wesley, numbers of men were his peers in faith. Butler, Toplady, Romaine, John Newton, and a whole host beside, got as firm a grip on what faith can reach, and said words as noble for it as he did. But Wesley had more *hopefulness* in his little finger than any other man of them had in his whole body, not excepting even Whitefield, who was always hampered by the chills and fever of Calvinism. Wesley was the liberal Christian apostle of his day, and his Methodism the liberal Christianity. His successors, however, have long since ceased to pull up stream. But so it was, that, wherever Wesley went, men caught the contagion of his great hope, and then ran tirelessly as long as they lived, kindling over all the world And so Macaulay does well to say, that no man can write a history of England in the last century, who shall fail to take into account Wesley's vast influence in the common English life.

This was what Paul had to begin with. How did he get it?

We are watching, just now in this country, the solution of a very weighty problem. It is this: How nearly can the tree of knowledge overshadow and overgrow the tree of life in our children, and we still endure to see it, without a revolution? We take them in their tender age, make them do an amount of head-work before they are through the high school, to say nothing of college, most of us revolt from in our prime. They grow thin and pale in the process, lose vitality — and what there is no better word for than *vim* — every year; and so, at last, they graduate, with a fine stock of knowledge, and an utter loathing of it in many cases; that is, half inanition and half intellectual dyspepsia.

In a deep, spiritual sense, this was what the world had come to in religion in Paul's time, and what Paul had come to when the great hope struck him on his way to Damascus. As a Jew, he had run after all the signs, miracles, and dogmas of his church; as a scholar, had dipped away down into what was known then of the nature and philosophy of things; and, alike as Pharisee and philosopher, he had been in awful and appalling earnest, only to find that somehow his heart was dead to all the good of it. It was then that the new hope had caught him, given him a new life, and made him seem like a crazy man to the Roman, as he went telling of the wonder. But as the chemist can keep you a piece of ice in a white-hot crucible, so in Paul's nature there was a place cooler than any thing the Roman suspected, where the worth of the new hope was calmly proven right along, and always with the same result,— that, wherever it took full possession, it opened the soul afresh to earth and heaven, started all sorts of new energies and activities, and, being a new life, made a new man.

Then, in life generally, as in religion particularly, this hope is essential. "Those sciences are always studied with the keenest interest," says Sir William Hamilton, "that are in a state of progress and uncertainty. Absolute certainty and completion would be the paralysis of any study; and the last and worst calamity that could befall man, as he is now constituted, would be the full and final possession of speculative truth he now vainly anticipates as the consummation of his happiness." And so it is always true, that the restless radicals in speculative theology, in any age, instead of being infidels, are saviours, because they bring in a new hope, and break in on the appalling dogma of a finality, with the news that yonder, away in the distance, is the intimation of a new world better and more beautiful than this the time lives in; and then, while a timid conservatism is crying out it is impossible, as did the conservatism of old Spain, they put out up stream, like Columbus, and find it.

I take no credit to the liberal faith we have no right to claim, when I say what I believe, that posterity will do us justice for endeavoring to save even the Bible from contempt in the mind of this age, — first, by showing a better truth in it than was allowed to exist in the dogmas of the churches; and, second, by affirming that there is an infinite truth over and above the Bible, into which all men are welcome to penetrate who will or can, — so opening the vista of a blessed and boundless hope to the always unsatisfied mind and soul.

Then I must make this general hope my own particular possession. Our time, and all time, abounds in those who have a great faith, but not a great hope; the solid certainty about the heart, but not the shining assurance about the intellect. God will make all right somehow, they feel; but tell them that he will do far more exceeding abundantly above all that they can ask or *think*, and that will strike them as something they never adequately realized, always providing they believe you Yet it is this alone that lifts us out of the world of inspection into that of expectation; that flashes into the soul the vision of that shy, trembling, blue, misty distance, on the far horizon of the world of grace and truth; hinting rather than revealing its beauty, but bringing untold treasure of rich experiences by the way, as we pull up stream to seek it, — experiences we had never suspected, staying down among the flats.

Friends, I would not like to think of heaven as in any sense a finality. If, when old Bunyan's Christian went in at those golden gates, he gave up a great hope for a great possession, — then, knowing what I do, and only what I do, I pity him.

Young men and women, with this life mainly before you, get this hope. I have had twenty years more of life than you have; and, if I could tell you some of it that can only be known where no secrets are hid, you would acknowledge it was as hard for me as it ever can be for you. I call back to you from my vantage-ground of twenty years, and beseech you to bring, with a great faith, a great hope; to make sure, that there is not a day you can live, bending over your work, with a sad sense perhaps that the life is going out of you in the merest necessity of living, but brings you nearer to some divine surprise of blessing, some great unfolding of God's very glory.

Men and women in middle life, as I am; with the bloom gone from some things that seemed very beautiful, as they lay glistening in the dew of the morning; with ashes for beauty, yonder in the cemetery; and with a dumb, daily care about things that must be cared for; with children growing up, for whose future you plan and pray; with a faith still in the things from which the bloom has gone, and that God, who has given you ashes for beauty, will some time give you beauty for ashes; that things will come right generally at last, and that the children will some time scramble into the right place as you did, — I charge you, as one to whom God has entrusted the keys, — the sense and faculty of realizing that his dark ways open, — to take for your helmet the hope of salvation. Whatever you do, never let a painful inspection rob you of a great expectation. If, as you live, you try to live faithfully, then, as the Lord liveth, try to live hopefully, or you will miss the better half of your living. Do you go to your graves these winter days, and observe how the flowers you tended there last summer are dead, and think of other and fairer dead, of which those were but the poor intimation. For the sake of all that can fill you with the everlasting life, open your heart to the sense of that spring-tide, sure to rise, when the sun comes back; and tell your soul, that is but the intimation also of the spring-tide poor David Gray sang about, as he lay a-dying, in the first bloom of his life, —

> "There is life with God
> In other kingdoms of a sweeter air:
> In Eden every flower is blown. Amen."

So may all sing, if to an inreaching faith they will add an outlooking hope, — will know that this flutter of the heart, that causes them to open their eyes wide, reaches for its fruition into certainties immutable as heaven.

VIII.

LOVE.

1 Cor. xiii. 13: "Now abideth faith, hope, charity, these three; but the greatest of these is charity."

It was my lot lately to speak to you about two prime things in our life, — Faith and Hope. One other thing still remains to be considered, — Love; in Paul's estimation, the essence of all professions and possessions in religion whatever. I want to speak to you of this greatest thing now; to try and tell you what it is, what it can do, and so what we are, if we possess it; and, by consequence, what we are not if we do not possess it, though we may have every thing beside that earth and heaven can give. In the text, the word is translated charity. It is a term that touches, at the best, only one little corner of love. In Wickliffe's time, however, from whose Bible this translation was adopted into our version, love and charity were as nearly related as charity and benevolence are now. This can be understood, if we will remember that charity and dear, in the sense of precious, belong to the one root. They spring from what was common enough when they were born, — dearth or scarcity. Food was then precious, much esteemed, much loved. The generation to which my grandfather belonged had some such idea as this. They lived through a time when a succession of bad seasons, and a wasteful war, had reduced the whole working population of England to miserable black bread. Then good bread, sound and white, was dear; not as it is now to us in money value merely, but in this primitive value of something to love, a small piece being given to the children sometimes on a Sunday, as a very precious thing.

In that way, we get at the old meaning of this word charity. Five hundred years ago, it was so understood generally, as to warrant its adoption by Wickliffe in preference to love. In that sense, Milton still uses it, three hundred years after, in "Paradise Lost," in the lines, —

> "Which of ye will be mortal, to redeem
> Man's mortal crime?
> Dwells in all heaven a *charity* so dear?"

And Dr. Samuel Clarke still later says, "Charity

doth not merely signify, as we use it now, almsgiving to the poor; but universal love and goodwill to all men." The word must have gone out of use as expressing love, however, at a very early day, — perhaps about the time when people ceased to put any love into their charity, making it merely a duty; for, a century only after Wickliffe, Coverdale renders the word as we have it, Cranmer follows Coverdale, and the Geneva Bible both. And I have dwelt this moment on the matter, — first, that you might see how it stands; and, second, that you may see something else that is not without importance, so long as we prefer the Bible in our worship before all other books.

A few Sundays ago, I read the lesson for the morning, a part of the Sermon on the Mount, from the translation of Andrews Norton, no doubt one of the best in existence; and, wherever it differs from the one we use, generally, the nearest right. I heard a number of comments afterward on the change. I did not hear one say it was for the better: everybody, on the whole, preferred the old version. So in my heart I do. I have read it ever since I read any thing, and my fathers before me for many generations. Our mothers read it as the sleeping babes nestled beside them; and, when the babes were old men of fourscore, and dying, the minister read it to the departing soul, and over the dust by the grave. And so no wonder it is in our hearts. But what about the head? We owe something to that. When the German peasant said to the priest, "I cannot repeat the Lord's Prayer, but I can give you the tune," he did precisely what we (who would have laughed at him) do every time that we prefer the sound to the sense, — the old familiar words, now only partly true, to the truth and life of Norton and Noyes. I think, if the term "villain" had been so fortunate as to be the best translation, at the time our version was made, of the word "servant," as it was in the elder English, and then the old sense had left it as it has, there would be great numbers of worshippers of the common version, quite ready to show what a sound, well-flavored word it is, especially if they were not servants. The truth is, the best equivalent for either Greek or Hebrew is always the English that can give me the keenest edge or the finest aroma of the original for which it stands; and, that word being the truest, is therefore the most sacred. So that not this, because it is old, or that, because it is new, but that which, with the letter, can transfer to me the spirit of the original, is the most sacred book.

This said, the question comes up for our consideration, What is this love, of which Paul makes such marvellous account? In the chapter in which my text occurs, he conducts one of the most striking arguments, by affirmation, ever made, to show what a supreme thing it is. He supposes himself possessing the finest qualities, excepting this one, that can be imagined. An eloquence so noble as to combine manly breadth with angelic insight, — I may have that, he says. Then he takes a brazen instrument and blows through it one of those discordances we have all heard from the thing, and says, If I have not love, my eloquence is that. Or I may be able to dive, by my intuitions, into the very heart of things (with Shakspeare, he would have said, if he were writing the Epistle now), or may hold in my brain the whole encyclopedia of human knowledge, and the result may be a power that can lift mountains out of their sockets; but, if I have not love, what I have and what I am is nothing. Nay, with all this I may combine a charity so boundless, as to leave me at last as poor as the poverty I have stripped myself to relieve; and a devotion so absolute, that I will be burnt at the stake. But eloquence, intuition, knowledge, faith, benevolence, and devotion, altogether, are merely so many ciphers, if I have not love.

Now, is this wonderful governing quality capable of being made simple and clear, like faith and hope, so that I may know inevitably whether I possess it? — must be a great question, if Paul is right, as no doubt he is. What, then, is this love? It is a word traceable altogether to many different roots. That could not be otherwise; because, in every rivulet that now makes this river of the English tongue, it must have been present in one form or other. Love would naturally be one of the very first things the most abject savages must find a name for, after getting a word to express each of the bare needs of life. The first time the man of the forest tried to win a maiden in some higher way than by the ancient contrivance of carrying her off by force, he would need the word. The first time the mother had to tell of the mysterious glow in her heart toward her babe in its helplessness, she would need the word. And so love, in one root, is longing; in another, goodness; in another, preference: but, to me, the right rests at last with Adam Clarke's idea, that it is the Teutonic word *leben*,— life. "This is *life*," these children of nature said, when they first began to be conscious of this glowing wonder in their hearts. "You are my life," the man said when he went to win the maiden; and the mother, when she caught her nursling to her heart. Love is to live; and not to love is not to live. And it was exactly the definition that John hit on away off across the world, when he wanted to tell of the nearest and dearest of all the relations the soul can hold to God.

And so, if you will recall what was said about faith,— that it is inreaching; and hope, that it is outlooking,— we come then to what we are to understand of love,— that it is *in being*. By faith I stand; by hope I soar; by love I am. Faith assures me, hope inspires me; love is me, at my best. "Love," says an old French lexicon, "is the sameness of souls." —"Love," says Luther, "is that by which I desire to be in perpetual union with that I love."—

7

"Love," says Dr. South, " is the spirit and spring of the universe." — " Love," says Emerson, " is our highest word and synonym of God." — " And love," says Solomon, " is strong as death." But, the instant we read that, we say Solomon does not reach the mark in his definition, any more than he did in his life; for, in the history of humanity, millions of proofs have been given that love is stronger than death, and is, as Erasmus says, " as immortal, when it is rooted in virtue, as virtue herself."

And it is only as we keep close to this idea and fact, — of love as life, — that we can prevent its being confounded with other and baser things, that, getting mixed up with it in our language, act like the baser metals mixed up in the coinage of a country, giving the real gold and silver a lower relative value, and debasing the whole fair standard of the commonwealth. Love, for example, is not lust. Because love, for whatever may in itself be good, adds just so much as there is in what I love to life; while lust for that very thing exhausts life. Here are two men devoted to money-making. In the one, money is a love; in the other, a lust. In the heart in which it is a love, it acts like a fire, expanding and softening; in the heart in which it is a lust, it acts like a frost, hardening and contracting. In Peabody and Peter Cooper, — and I wish to heaven I could put some noble Chicago man into the catalogue, — in men like these it is a love. Their hearts grow with their growing fortunes. They are solid men; they do solid things, — found great libraries and institutes, inaugurate noble movements for model dwellings for the poor, while, at the same time, they are sustaining vast commercial interests, that make the difference between Glasgow and Cork.

But, in numbers we have all known or heard of, the love of money is a lust, and acts like a frost, hardening, contracting, and finally killing every large idea and generous impulse in their souls. They will say the money is my own, to do as I like. It is only their own, as if they owned a glacier that was for ever accumulating over them, and lived at the bottom of one of its chasms. Their money is their own, as that ice would be their own, — it is their shroud and coffin and grave. When we say money is the root of all evil, we mean lust of money. So long as you

can be sure that the fortune you are making is
" expanding with the expanding soul," you may
be sure that it is only good, and that continually;
because it is so much added to your life, now
and for ever. The love of money to the lust of
money is as the preparation for heaven and hell.

This is still more clearly true, when we touch
another thing, about which we never think of
speaking as the love of this or that, even though
we put such an affix to the love of God ; but consider it enough just to say the word, and it tells
the whole tale. The most primitive idea of the
relation of the man and woman in our Bible is
not at all what we make it now, — that the man
is the volume and the woman the supplement. It
is rather that the man is the first volume, good
enough as far as it goes ; but, if there is to be no
second, more aggravating than if there wasn't
any, — a story half told and then broken off just
as we began to get interested, demanding not a
supplement but a complement, to make it complete. So the thing stands in the first Hebrew
dawn of time. The man is as good as the Lord
can make him ; but *then* there is nothing for even
the divine Worker to do but put him to sleep

until he makes a woman. And the first thing he tells him about her, as he bids them join their hands, is, that she shall stand to him in the line of that love which is life,—shall not be somebody else, but his own intimate self, as he hers; soul blending with soul, and becoming one, as two drops of dew become one in the heart of a flower-cup. It is so for ever with all true love.

When the young man, living in a room, eating in a restaurant, and troubled about more things than ever Martha was, feels at last how contracted and poor such a life is at the best, and says in his heart, "This is not living: I must get me a wife,"—whatever may be his idea of the wife he wants, the word he uses to describe his condition reaches away into the truth. It is not living: it is just half living, and probably not that. His heart is crying out for the rest of his life.

Or when the maiden teaching school, working in the store, helping to keep house at home, doing whatever a maiden may do, thinks of a question that might be asked and an answer that might be given, if all was right that seems most wrong,—she is dreaming of another life, in which a double care and sorrow and pain is only another name for a deeper color, a more exquisite texture, and a double warp and woof running through the whole web of her future existence. That is the love which is life, — the love whereby the two becoming one doubles the intrinsic value of each for ever.

But there is that calling itself love which is lust, — something that seeks not a life, but an appanage to life, and reaps for its sowing a harvest of gray ashes. Love informs life; lust exhausts it. Love is the shining sun, lust is the wandering star. When I remember some sights I have seen, — how men and women have mistaken lust for love, and then, when they had found out their mistake, have gone on dragging their chain, biting it, and growing ever more bitter the longer they live, — I have wanted to lift up my voice like a trumpet, to show men and women this distinction, so that it shall be for ever unmistakable; and to cry to young men and maidens, especially, that hear me, "How can ye escape, if ye neglect so great salvation?"

But, beside such special applications, there is no direction in which we can turn but this spirit meets us with its sweet, solemn face, demanding to be put in the van of our endeavor, or there can be no wonder and glory of success. Consider the lesson we have learned in our war. When we plunged into that red sea, the gentlemen of England were looking on. They stated frankly their opinions,— a few on one side; a multitude on the other. The few said we should hold our own: they were sure of it,— John Bright, Thomas Hughes, John Forster, of Bradford, and all the men after their heart. The great multitude which no man can number said we had gone under. The "Times" thundered — the "Saturday Review" sneered, and M.P.'s made conclusive addresses to the Honorable House on the failure of democratic institutions. What made this difference among men of about equal opportunity? I will tell you. John Bright, Thomas Hughes, John Forster, and all that stood in their company, loved us with a love that made their hearts throb and their souls sing; so that Faith stood square, and Hope plumed her wings, and they became the glad ministers of their leader and guide. And what made other men, whose names I will not celebrate by this momentary mention, sure it was all over? It is the weakest word I can find, when I say they did not love us. They had no faith in us and no hope for us, because they had no love; " for now remaineth faith, hope, love, these three; but the greatest of these is love." It is entirely possible, that, in the beginning, they might not differ very much in their conclusions; but as somewhere on this continent the water parts on the two sides of a barn, — this way to sunshine and freedom; that to the fetters of frost, — so the two orders of men were positive and negative. And as the days went on the love was life, but the want of it death.

When a man really loves a land and a cause, it piles great stores of life into his heart; so that he may even come to some dreadful pass where faith and hope fail him, and yet love shall carry him through. One morning, when I was in Europe, I had two things present themselves to be done. It was in Lucerne. Louis Napoleon had come the night before with the empress. They could be seen; or there was an old bridge to be seen, on which the good city had painted some of the most notable things in her history. I neglected the emperor, but I saw the bridge:

and here is one of the stories it had to tell. Hundreds of years ago, that Austria, now shorn of the strength she so prostituted, went into Switzerland to devour *her* bit of freedom, — burnt the harvests, besieged the cities, and prepared to crush out the band that armed to oppose her. There was little room for faith or hope in such a contest; but then all the more room for an utterly limitless love. You know the story. The enemy advanced, a solid wall of steel, and began to creep round the little band. Switzer after Switzer fell trying to break in and turn the tide of battle. There might be hope only if the wall was broken, and the peasants could come within the line. Then, in the last dreadful moment, one went rushing, for love of Switzerland, on the solid ranks of the spears, broke the close array, by gathering them into his own breast, — that is what they show you painted on the panels of the old bridge at Lucerne, and I have never regretted going to fill my heart afresh with it, instead of going to see the Emperor: it was the chance of getting a look at a mortal or an immortal. I went to see the immortal, — to see the shrine of the man who had the love which is life so strong in his heart, that his life itself is still in its prime, after almost five hundred years.

And this is the truth about our life, in whatever way we test it. The love which is life alone can make life all it must be, whatever we may be and do beside. When the father wants to put his son on the way to success, if he is a wise man, he most anxiously tries to find out where the lad's love lies; for there, he knows, he will have faith and hope, because the love will be a perpetual inspiration and motive, a perpetual life, to duty and accomplishment: while, to put him at what he can never love, will only exhaust and disgust him, until at last it is given up in despair. Not that the boy and man is not faithful and dutiful, but just because he could not make up his mind to die out by a constant drain on all the power and vitality there was in him, when there is still a hope that he can do that which will be like a well of water springing up into everlasting life. Nay, so true this is, that if one lad with love in his heart fails to do the thing he loves, while another with what he thinks is love, but which is only lust, of fame or fortune, shall in a measure succeed, — the loving heart shall still be fullest of the life of the endeavor. Hazlitt, as a painter, had this love: Haydon had lust. Hazlitt never succeeded in painting a picture, after all his endeavors; but he did succeed in loving his art so, that its power and life lifted his soul into the finest insight and appreciation of pictures possessed by any man in his time: while poor Haydon, perpetually lusting for applause, and to be the founder of a great school, and to be honored and worshipped, went on in an ever more desperate and deadly exhaustion, down to his death.

So I would love to linger in these regions of the common life, if there was time, and open more fully to you this almost endless application of love as life. But there is one great application remaining, — this that Paul makes, which is but another way of saying this that the Almighty makes; for the words of men that speak as they are moved by the Spirit do not create the thing: they simply reveal it.

And the task is the more easy, because these things. I have tried to make clear are most intimately one with this that remains; so that you do not turn away from these to come to this, but just work on, facing in the one direction, getting nearer and nearer to your study, to find in the very centre of it this that the apostle fills so full of all that is greatest and best. For, no doubt, when the distinction is drawn in which a man is made as eloquent as men and angels together, and wise as all the seers, and accomplished as all the scholars, and benevolent to the last mite in his possession, and devoted as the martyr at the stake, yet is deemed to be nothing if he have not love, it is the line between love and lust that is drawn; between doing a thing in order to get to heaven, and doing a thing because we are already heavenly; between being religious for what may come of it, and expressing what has come, as naturally as a child expresses its joy by laughter.

It is charged to our faith, sometimes, that it is indifferent about a change of heart. Let a man do the works, it is said (we say), and then he is sure to be right. It may be sometimes true: it is as possible for us to fall into a cold morality as any other order of religious believers. It is a very great mistake, however, to suppose that, because we are not eternally opening the doors and poking the fire, we are therefore indifferent as to whether it is burning. We can no more believe that a man can live this life, which is love, and do its work for God and man, and make a grand success of it, by doing good or handsome or charitable or religious things, expecting that they will somehow at last work their way into the heart, and make all right,— than we can believe that a locomotive can be started right, filled full of power, and sent on its way, rejoicing as a strong man to run a race, by kindling a fire about it instead of *in the firebox*. It is for ever indispensable, and for every body, that they have a change of heart, if they need one. If in the soul there is no glow and expansion,— no such feeling in the heart as that which you may understand easily, any time, you will watch a mother in the midst of her little brood of children,— then there must be such a glow and expansion, or all there is beside is sounding brass and a tinkling cymbal. "He that loveth not, knoweth not God." It is the old, sweet, single word, without the affix, as when we speak of the love of the man and maiden. "He that loveth not, knoweth not

God." The very love of God is only one of the loves in our loving. It is not the object but the life of which I am to make sure; and then, as Richter says, "the heart in this heaven, like the wandering sun, sees nothing, from a dew-drop to an ocean, but a mirror it warms and fills." "So loving was St. Francis," says Ruskin, "that he claimed a brotherhood with the wolf." —"So loving was St. Francis," says another, "that he remembered those that God had seemingly forgotten." It is this love, and this alone, that "beareth all things, believeth all things, hopeth all things, endureth all things, and never faileth."

But do you say, "Oh! tell me how to get this love?" I tell you, you have the first white spark of it. If you really love at all, if you love a dog, you have that in your heart which may grow to be as mighty as the love of the first archangel. If I can love that I do love with the love which is life, — with a true heart, fervently, — as I open my heart to this grace and goodness of loving, the breath of heaven will draw through and fan the flame, kindling this way and that, until the whole soul is on fire with a love that warms and energizes whatever it touches, like the pure sun. It is a divine life, but its kindling is in a human love. Who has not pondered that wonderful history? One goes to a wedding. Only his mother knows much about him: it is possible he knows but little about himself. He sits apart from the merry-making: there is not much there that he cares for; but at last there is one thing, — the bridegroom, an old friend probably, is about to be ashamed and humiliated to the whole country-side. He saves him from that shame and humiliation. I care not a pin about whether it was water or wine they had; but here, at the opening of a gospel, is the story of one who, for "auld lang syne," will not let his friend hang his head ashamed. It is the first spark to be detected of the greatest fire that ever burned in a soul. Once started it caught, — here a cripple, there a blind man; here a widow, weeping by the bier of her only son; there a madman wandering among the graves: leaping from one to another, growing white and full, deep and intense, with what it fed on, until it burnt through the very asbestos of the grave, and made uncounted millions of hearts burn with the power

of an endless life. It was a love which is life
that kindled the flame; and it was what we may
all realize in some good measure, if we will. Then
we may be able to say no word to which the
world will listen; may have no faculty, possess
no knowledge; be as poor as the widow with her
two mites, which made one farthing; and believe
that we do not believe any thing. But, because
we *love* with the love which is life, we shall have
the eloquence which surpasses speech, and the
intuition that dives below the faculty of the
seers; the knowledge before which the lamp of
knowledge pales, as a taper before the sun; the
gold which is good, and the devotion that is
better than burning, — the devotion of loving.
Heaven will then be in the soul: we shall
not *seek* it: we shall *carry* it. For as " now we
see through a glass darkly, but then face to
face; and as now we know in part, but then we
shall know as we are known," so " now abideth
faith, hope, love, these three; but the greatest of
these is *Love*."

IX.

ASCENDING AND DESCENDING ANGELS.

JOHN i. 51: "The angels of God ascending and descending upon the Son of man."

THAT is, the angels come from below the Son of man, as well as from above him; yet they are the angels of God, from whatever quarter they come. And as in space the heavens are all about us, — not above only, but below; so in the soul the heavens enfold the son of man every way, and below him, as above him, open to his angels.

The term "son of man," in the broad sense, has no mystical meaning. It reaches clean through the scale of life, from the son of man a reptile in the Book of Job, and the son of man as grass in the Book of Isaiah, to the Son of man Lord of the sabbath, the Son of man, with power on earth to forgive sins, and the Son of man glorified of the Gospels. So it is at once the general title for any child of humanity, and the one name Jesus Christ always claims for himself. "The

Son of man," therefore, is not only the loftiest, but the lowest man. From the reptile to the Redeemer, it embraces every one.

But, broad as this term is, it is not broader than this of the angels that come from the open heavens everywhere into his life; meaning, in the simplest sense, that which is actively at work; and, in the sacred sense, that which is doing God's will. For there is no trace anywhere of an indolent angel. You follow the term carefully as it is used by these Bible men, and find that it is by no means confined to what we understand by "angels" commonly; but they seem to believe, with one of their own rabbins, that "all divine operations, whether natural or spiritual, are done by angels. Jacob's ladder is everywhere stretching from earth to heaven, and every grass-blade has its own angel to attend it."

And so you will find, that, excepting the angel is never feminine, there is almost infinite diversity of angelhood. They are gods, and sons of God, and men; the spirit of the thunder and wind and fire; the spirit of nations, kings, statesmen, and pastors. Time would fail me to tell of their almost endless diversity, — from the angel standing at the gate of Eden, whose sword flamed every way before the paradise lost, to the angel with the golden reed, who measures the city in the paradise regained. The Bible conception of the angel touches, on one side, the spirits that stand nearest the immanent glory; and, on the other, that mystery of life in which —

> "Every clod feels a stir of might,
> An instinct within it that reaches and towers,
> And, feeling blindly toward the light,
> Climbs to a soul in grass and flowers."

And I have made this brief study of the Bible senses of the "son of man" and the "angels," because I suppose you have hardly imagined what a breadth and scope these terms take; and also because, in this inclusiveness, we can find applications of my text it is hopeless to seek in the common conception of what it means. Read it in the light of the commentaries usually written about angels, and you say at once, "Here is something that relates entirely to the Messiah. It is a part of that whole system of things that makes him rather the exception than the instance of humanity. These angels were to minister, and did minister, to him, because he was Messiah, not because he was man; and so we have no part or lot in the matter, except to study the curious records of their nature and agency, contained in the far-away hints of Gospel and Epistle. We live now in a prosy railroad world, in which the telegraph can outstrip in swiftness the swiftest flying angel of the old ages; and angels, for many a century now, have fled from the earth." This is all easily said, and men are saying it on all sides of us. But it is not true that the angels never come: the trouble is, we do not look for them where they are. We look for them to sweep down through the opening heavens when they have come down already, and are hidden in the bluebells at our feet. We want them to appear like the great angels of Angelo: they are looking at us out of the dreamy wandering eyes of the babe born yesterday. We read of the angel that came and fought for Israel in the old days. He came and fought for us in these new days, not on wings, but on strong tramping feet; black, but comely; standing side by side with our brothers and sons. He strikes the rock in the wilderness now with a drill, and bores Artesian wells, and ministers to hunger and agony through a woman's hands and heart, and a surgeon's skill, and all common human agencies. Are they not all ministering spirits sent out to minister? But —

> "I think we do as little children do,
> Who lean their faces on the window pane,
> To sigh the glass dim with their own breath-stain,
> And shut the sky and landscape from their view."

This indicates, then, the direction of my thought. It is not to teach you some strange doctrine, but to insist that you stand true to an old doctrine. I want not to bar out of any life the loftiest ministry of angelhood, but to insist also on your recognition of the lowest; and that these come to us also. Do you say that Moses and Elias came and talked with Jesus? Admitted. But the children he took in his arms were angels too, whose ministry was as indispensable to his tried and lonely life as that of the ascended prophets. And Martha troubled about his dinner, and Mary washing his feet with her tears, — these were angels as truly as those that found him wandering in the wilderness, and fainting in the garden.

Small matters, you say, to that high soul, — a batch of children, a woman in a tiff, and a woman in tears; surely you are lowering the standard under which the angels muster, when you make these angels. We can think how these others might sweep down through the blue to his side, to minister unto him. But women and children, so far below him,— how can they be angels? These ascended, as those descended upon the Son of man. Indeed, it is wonderful to notice what a great part these angels that ascend play in the development of the life and truth as it is in Jesus; or it would be wonderful, if we did not see all about us now, how clear it is, that, when a life has trued itself to divine standards fairly, then whatever comes to it is somehow transmuted into fine gold for its service. To me, the shadow in the life of Jesus is only less inestimable than the light; the most adverse things seem to be as indispensable as the most felicitous. His homelessness, his loneliness, his hindrances, his sufferings,— all come trooping from below, hard, black, forbidding in the distance; but, when they light on him, they are angels. We love him more because he had not where to lay his head, than if he had been lodged in the palace of the Herods. We could never have had some of the most priceless things in the Gospels, but for the fierce bigotry of Scribe and Pharisee, vexing his righteous soul. The very Prodigal is made a minister to the most pregnant illustration in the Gospels of God's great mercy; while the lost woman stands for the most touching instance of his own great humanity. Nay, the heartless priest and Levite cannot escape. the mighty transmutation; and the darkest, saddest, most deplorable event in time, — his agony and cruel death, — is the most significant, the very central circumstance, in the history of man. Now, these things, and all things like them, as they come up about the Son of man, are compelled into a divine service. Whatever the thing may be, it is no matter: when once it touches him, it becomes an angel. From the lowest to the highest, from above and from below, their nature always waits to be revealed in the nature of the man to whom they come.

Right here, however, the question meets us, What son of man now has any right to expect such a ministry of angels in his life, as this that was identified with the life of the Saviour? We cannot hope for it, because we can bear no such responsibility on the one hand, and can claim no such worthiness on the other. There is but one answer to this objection. It is, that not what we may be worth to ourselves or the world, but what we are worth to God, being the prime reason why the angels come at all, we cannot be sure that there is no such ministry except we were sure there is no such worth. It would seem clear enough, that the wretched man who gets drunk, beats his wife and starves his children, would have no hope of an angel; but he has perhaps a houseful pleading with him and ministering to him every day, because, bad as he is, he is not the son of perdition, but a son of man. When your son has grown to be a man, and you can order his steps no longer, it may then be his destiny to go to some place a mile south of his home; but, in his wild wilfulness, he turns his face north, and then it is seven and twenty thousand miles of weary travelling to get there. Will the angel of your love ever leave him; or will his weariness and pain and sorrow be only a curse to him? It is a horrible thing to teach that the Almighty made even the fiends only to torment us, to lead us wrong and lure us down; and then, at last, to listen while they send up yells of fierce laughter over our hapless misery. What I do I must stand by; no doubt of that, if I will not take refuge in the infinite pity and pardon. The wages of sin is death,— death when the sin is done, death right along; the deadening and darkening of all I might have been, had I done right right on. But, when the angels above me are powerless; when my mother's love, and my father's faith, and wife and children and friends, all fail; when all the great influences from heaven fail, and I *will* rush on and down,— then the angels come from below, in terrible shapes perhaps, and armed with dire torments: but they come to save me, and mean to save me.

Still the other is the nobler application. When a man is on the right way, his heart open to heaven, his life a prayer to be right; is longing right, striving right, and fighting, like Bunyan's Christian, up and down; and who, though he may plunge into fits of despond, and wander in shadows of death, and get locked up in dungeons of despair, will never, if he know it, turn his back on the one right way,— on *this* son of man the angels descend in constant grace; and even the things that come from below and appal him, when once the knight has well fought his battle, are turned into forms of beauty, the daughters of the king.

And be sure I do not mean by all this, merely that elemental properties, and providential occurrences, and men good and bad, and nature in her glory and grandeur and terror, are the only angels that attend such a life, coming from below and above to be its ministers. I do mean all these. I can see how tribulation, and persecution, and famine, and nakedness, and peril, and sword, and life, and death, and principalities, and powers, and things present, and things to come, *may* all be ministering angels; but I cannot strip life of loftier influences than these, that are yet lower than the incoming of the Holy Ghost.

I have a friend, for instance, who is so sure that the child gone out of her arms comes back to her as a ministering angel, that the belief wins her out of her mourning, and fills her, I know, with a perfect peace. Now, who am I that I shall say, " My friend, you are mistaken"? I watch the eyes of this son of man, and see them fill with the light of heaven, as he recognizes the presence of spiritual things I can only see distantly and dimly or not at all. Who am I that I should say, " What you see as a person, I see as a principle; and I am right, and you are wrong"? I know, as well as Newton did, that two and two make four; that is a principle, it is plain to both of us. But I stumble and stand stricken at the portals of a world in the line of that principle, that opens to him into an infinite beauty and goodness. Yet, because I cannot see what he can see, shall I say, " You are the victim of geometrical imaginations; there is nothing beyond simple addition?" As I show most wisdom when I sit at the feet of the master in geometry, and accept his revelation, inasmuch as it is deeper and better than my own; so I show most wisdom when I sit at the feet of this Master, who has most insight into spiritual things, listening reverently to what he can tell me; whose powers so far surpass my own.

So, in this loftiest sense, I cannot strip the world of angels, and send them back into dim and distant ages.

> "I think the sudden joyance, that illumes
> A child's mouth sleeping, unaware may run
> From some soul newly loosened from earth's tombs;
> I think the passionate sigh, which, half begun,
> I stifle back, may reach and stir the plumes
> Of some tall angel standing in the sun."

But this insisted on, — that wonderful spiritual powers, of the loftiest order, are all about my life, only hidden because that is best. There waits that vaster order of ministers which includes whatever beside can be an angel. And, in naming these finally, I cannot do better than follow the track of illustration I have already made, and say, that to us, as to our great forerunner, whatever influences in the world and in life touch us to the quick, whether they come from below or from above, if we are in the line of divine laws and leadings, are all ascending or descending angels.

The little child comes, with its crumb of utterly helpless humanity. And, if it were possible to be purely impersonal spectators, I suppose there would be no greater wonder on the earth than the almost infinite patience of the mother with its habits, ailments, and, if it were not just what it is, its endless annoyances. Yet in that one small thing is hidden both angels. It is not the smile she gets; not the wealth of beauty she sees, thank God, whether the world can see it or no; not the freshness of its opening life, — not these only, these angels from above; but its very waywardness and greediness, its fractiousness and sleeplessness, develop in her nature deep springs of love, that could never come out of its absolute perfection. From below as well as from above, the angel comes to all true mothers from all children; and no mother can afford to lose one of these ministries.

And as the life grows in us, the angels still come from either hand. Our home is holy; good angels are always lighting on it out of heaven: but we leave it, as Jacob did, before we find out all about its angelhood. When the lad gets into the wilderness, with a stone for his pillow, then only he is for the first time aware of both the angels. And, in the full tide of the life of a son of man, sturdily bent on fighting the good fight clean through, the angels are everywhere. Let the young man keep himself pure, be the man he ought to be and can be, and then the woful painted shams on our streets, instead of being a danger and a snare, will even come to be a means of grace; for they will fill him with a great, sorrowful, manly pity, that ever one, who was some mother's child and is some man's sister, should lose so dismally her glory and her crown. Nay, he will be more human at the thought of the inhumanity that has made her what she is; and, instead of sneering at all women because she is so fallen, — as if a fool should sneer at the constellations because of the falling stars, — when God shall wake him out of his sleep, and say, " Behold the woman that I have made for thee!" he will reverence her with a more sacred reverence, and love her with a holier love.

Indeed, I know of no way in which a man or woman, determined toward whatsoever things are true, will not find the angels climbing up as well as coming down to him. What, I pray you, had Luther been, had all Christendom come over to his side the moment he launched his thesis; or Cromwell, had there been no Naseby or Marston Moor? What had Wesley been as Archbishop of Canterbury, or Washington as the bosom-friend of George the Third? What had Howard been but for the prisons that were a disgrace to the worst ages, or Lady Russell but for the martyrdom of her husband, or Florence Nightingale but for the Circumlocution Office? Not that these things are there, that the man or woman may reap renown; but being there, and they right in their track and true to the duty they present, they find, in some way, that what was in the doing the hardest and saddest thing in their life was still so transmuted in the process as to become an angel. So a shaking bog in Lancashire ministered to Stephenson, and the water flowed for Fulton, and the lightning flashed for Franklin, and the steam hissed for Watt, and the electric fluid pulsed for Morse. So mere pigments and chemicals come up and meet in Hunt and Church, the angels of inspiration that come down; then, from the sons of God and the daughters of men, again other angels are born, that stand on the canvas, a glory and a praise.

It will be very pleasant and good that every man in this church succeed in his calling. It is indispensable that the very hardnesses and hindrances that rise up to appal him shall, by his right determination, turn to ministering angels. And I can hardly trust myself to say what angels couch in the saddest places of our life, — in the sick-room, by the deathbed, in the shadows of a sore disappointment, in the hope deferred that maketh the heart sick, in the very dungeons of despair. We shrink and shudder, and say, " I shall go down to my grave mourning." But some morning, all at once, we bethink us of the little key called *promise;* and it opens the dungeon door, and we creep out, blinking sadly into the sun. But there is the sun, sure enough, and we had thought he would never shine again; and here are the green pastures, and there the shining river. And men and women look at us with a new tenderness, because our lot has been so sad. Then the song sings itself somehow again; and, while we would shrink and shudder just as much next time, we cannot but discover how, in our very griefs, there were hidden angels reaching up to hide, within the dark experience, some treasure of patience or trust we could never have possessed, had the angels only descended on us, and our life been one long joy.

And I know, when I say all this, that I speak to common experience through the whole range of this angelhood. I think we do not begin to realize as we ought what ministries cluster round our life, to aid us in being what we may be, — angels, angels, every one, thick about us every day, bearing us in their hands, and lifting us up when we are fallen. Their faces gladden us when we do well, and grow very sad at us when we sin. Ay, and in some way those that we speak of and think of as in heaven love us still with all the old love of earth, and all the new love of heaven together. So, because they love us still, we are still one, our souls are in theirs, and they in ours. We touch hands in the spirit, and the light that is not the light of the sun covers and enfolds us all.

X.

THE FEAR OF GOD.

1 Peter ii. 17 : "Fear God."

I want to say, as an introduction to this sermon, that no writer or speaker in the Bible begins his revelation by trying, first of all, to prove that there is a God. In no part of the Bible is such proof ever attempted. These men appear to believe that the question is settled in some other way than by reasoning; or they feel that trying to prove the being of God is a lower thing than that which they are sent to do; or they are so filled with a great sense of his presence, that they do not believe it possible for a sensible man to doubt about his being, any more than to doubt about the sunlight on a summer's day, — living in a focus of belief, like that man who, brought before the Parliament of Toulouse on the charge of atheism, lifted a straw from the ground, and, holding it up before his accusers, said, "This straw compels me to believe that there is a God." But, while these men all believe that there is a God, they disagree very widely about his nature and character, and how he is related to man. To one he is a terror and perplexity, to another a supreme love; to one a power beyond all power, to another a limited, struggling principle; to one a grim Eastern despot, to another a forgiving Father, — his face beaming with love to this man, but to that man black with vindictive vengeance. A great deal of the trouble that men come to in trying to reconcile these things as they are found in the Bible, lies in their utter antagonism, and they can never be reconciled for that reason: therefore we can only take them as we find them, and test them by the truth itself. I intend to do this, as far as I am able, in the discussion of that character of God by which we are bidden to *fear* him. I think there are some thoughts of the fear of God that we may well ponder. I propose to name some hurtful and some useful fears of God common among men to-day, and to point out their value in the human life.

I. There is, first of all, a fear of God which

to me appears to be a reproduction, measure, or color of the national life, different as the nations differ. I believe it is impossible to bring a Frenchman and a German, or a Scotchman and an Irishman, or any two men that reach back into a radical difference of race, to regard God in the same way. Indeed we see this difference in two children of the same family. One child will rebel and take the penalty, snap his fingers and do it again; while another will tremble and shrink and fear. One will say prayers, and brood over those mysterious promptings of the soul that seem like the audible whispers of angels to some children; while another will appear to be shut altogether out of this heaven, revelling in the fresh new life of the present with a wealth of enjoyment past all telling, — "of the earth, earthy." So there are nations that are lightsome, careless, earthy, objective; and nations that are deep, stern, solemn, subjective; and the national nature colors the great central idea of God.

Where the father in the home is a fear, the God above is a fear. Where the father is careless, light-hearted, easily bought off, blending laughter and tears, smiles and frowns, a kiss and a blow, there the Holy Mother can turn the tides of fate, and the Friar make a good thing out of what, to a deeper-hearted people, is the dreadful, steady, immaculate justice. The Frenchman who could not stay to morning mass, but left his card upon the altar, flashed a light across the world that revealed the real texture of the French soul as vividly as you shall see it, if you watch for a year in the church of the Madeline, in Paris. And when the Scotchman went away from the kirk, for the first time in his life, to hear an Episcopal service, in which a fine organ played a prominent part, and said, as he came away, "Oh! it's verra bonnie; but it's an awfu' way of spending the Sabbath," he touched the deep, stern Scottish character — that, as some one has said, " delights to praise the Lord by singing infinitely out of tune" — better than it could be touched in a volume of disquisition.

So, friends, in a broad, national way, we take the thing that is nearest us to touch the infinite.

The glass through which we see God is darkened by our own breath. Some shadow of the dark or bright we cast of our own free will. But more than all that is this primitive, mysterious shadow of the race, — the shadow cast by blood and climate and circumstance, determining for all men — save, it may be, one in a thousand — whether their Supreme shall be revealed in the thunders of Sinai, or the sorrows of Olivet, or the glories of Zion, — a power that waits on our birth to take us up and mould us, and which smiles to hear us say, " What I will be I will." For as you may find the Soldanella Alpina, piercing through the snows upon the lower Alps, leaning its frail purple blossom over the fearful icy clefts, and the Victoria Regia in the hot lagoons of the South, opening her vast, shining petals to glisten in the sun, but never the great lily on the mountain, or the blue bell in the lake ; so the idea of God is moulded, more or less, by the great ranges of the race, the intimate life-blood of the country and the providence.

> " The Ethiop's god has Ethiop's lips,
> Black cheek and woolly hair,
> And the Grecian god a Grecian face,
> As keen-eyed, cold, and fair."

II. But, in our own nation, where so many nativities centre, the idea of God and the consequent fear of God differ very greatly. And I have thought that it might be of use to you, that I should note some forms of that fear as it exists all about us, and tell you what I think is a false and degrading, then what is a true and elevating, fear of God, for us here, and to-day.

The first and lowest form is a fear of God as a jailer and executioner, who stands and waits until that sure detective, Death, shall hunt the criminal down, and bring him into court (where, by the way, there is no jury, — a thing that certainly would not be omitted if these Western nations had written the Bible), and where, really without trial, — for his condemnation is a foregone conclusion, — he is turned into the despair and torment of the lost. This is the low, coarse, hell-fire fear, — the fear described in a quotation that every preacher of this school can repeat to you as readily as he can repeat the beatitudes, and that is sure to find a place in the revival season, which indeed would be incomplete without it. The writer is describing a death-bed, and tells you, —

> "In that dread moment, how the frantic soul
> Raves round the walls of her clay tenement;
> Runs to each avenue, and shrieks for help,
> But shrieks in vain! How wishfully she looks

> On all she's leaving, now no longer hers!
> A little longer, yet a little longer,
> Oh might she stay to wash away her stains,
> And fit her for her passage!
> Her very eyes weep blood, and every groan
> She heaves is big with horror; but the foe,
> Like a stanch murderer steady to his purpose,
> Pursues her close through every lane of life,
> Nor misses once the track, but presses on;
> Till, forced at last to the tremendous verge,
> At once she sinks to everlasting ruin."

Now, if you can bring a man to believe this, and to believe that God is to this dreadful penalty what the soul is to the body, what the burning is to the fire, the very life of the eternal torture, replying "Never, never, never" to every cry out of the pit of "Oh, when will this agony be over?" — then you have a fear of God in that man beside which the fear of a slave toward a cruel driver is a pleasant, frisky thing; and such a fear, when it strikes root in a man, can have but one of two results: it places him in a bitter, hopeless, blasphemous atheism, such as you often find in isolated communities that have heard only these dreadful teachers; or it forces him into a slavish, crouching, abject submission, where every free and noble aspiration is lost in the one great hunger to be on good terms with such a dreadful master. The Pagan, on this plane of belief, is wiser than the Christian. He says boldly, that the doer of this is the *evil* spirit, and so he tries to be on good terms with him. But wherever such a fear has a real place in the soul of man or woman, African, Indian, or Saxon, in that soul the love of God, or even a true fear of God, is utterly out of the question. It destroys every fair blossom of the soul ; it leaves nothing to ripen, — nothing beautiful, even to live.

III. Then, to the eye of the resolute Christian thinker, — who dares not, as Coleridge has said, " love even Christianity better than the truth, lest he shall come to love his own sect better than Christianity, and at last himself better than all," — there is another form of the fear of God, not the best by far, but far better than this utterly slavish fear. I mean that in which God becomes the embodiment of pure bargain, exacting from us, to the uttermost penny or the uttermost quivering nerve, whatever is due, — no more, no less. Here God appears with the guards and sanctities of the law about him, self-imposed and self-respected. The man need not contract the debt if it does not please him ; but, if he does contract it, he must pay, or another

must pay for him. Then the son of the great
creditor gives his own body to the knife, and
bears the intolerable agony instead of the debtor.
Now there is a touch of sublimity in this con-
ception. I do not wonder that Paul, standing
where he did, should be so filled with enthusiasm
by it, and should run all over the world to tell it,
with strong crying and tears. To Paul, educated
in the belief that a sacrifice was imperative, this
was a wonderful revelation, — the awful debt
paid, — paid by the Son in the gift of his life.
And to-day this form of the fear of God — even
where it makes the man into a wretched, shiftless
debtor, and God into a stern creditor, yet with
such infinite deeps of tenderness in his heart, that
he will give his own Son for us all — creates a
far nobler issue than that in which Antonio must
quiver in agony for ever, if for no debt of his
own, then for a debt contracted by his remotest
ancestor. There is that in this idea, which has
carried a wonderful weight with it, — such a fear
has its own touch of tender reverence. Convince
a man that this is true, and he will be awe-
stricken and inspired to some fearful love. The
life and death that hangs on such conditions

must be of vast importance, and a God at once so relentless and so merciful cannot be slighted.

Yet when we come to question the system, it will not stand. The moment you open the idea with the master-key of the Fatherhood of God, you begin to see that it cannot be true. It is the father punishing the brother who is innocent for the brother who is guilty. And you cannot help seeing, that, however willing the brother may be to bear, it is against the nature of true greatness in the father to inflict the penalty. It is no more *right* to do so, than it was right to punish the French page for the fault of the French prince. If you admit the principle, you do so at the expense of the clearest ideas of justice that are found in your own soul, and that guide you in every other decision. Either the doctrine must be wrong in some radical way, or the ideas that are right in every thing beside are wrong in this. If it was right that Christ should bear your sins in his own body on the tree, according to the common interpretation of that doctrine, it will be right for you to punish the elder child in your home the next time the younger breaks into some mad freak of temper. Besides, this doing wrong with the sure conviction that some one must suffer for it, and then crouching down behind another while he bears the blow; this running into a debt that you are sure another will have to pay; this lying on the shady side of the barn all through the summer, because you know you can beg enough corn to put you through the winter, from the man who toils all day in the hot sun, and who loves you so well, good, merciful man that he is, that you are sure he will not let you starve,—does *not* appear to me to be the best way to promote a stout, deep, steady, personal manliness. If you take the principle out of the realm of religious ideas, and bring it into common life, as a rule, it makes a man small, tricky, and vicious. Then this unlimited promise to pay creates all sorts of unfair and unsound debts. When the common run of men believe that they can have all they ask for, they are not likely to be particular about pennies. Our government is cheated every day in the exact ratio of the confidence of depraved rogues, that they can get their claims pulled through, and the better the man to indorse the claim, the more they will put down. If a good man will say this is all right when it is all wrong, they will slide in another cipher with perfect assurance. Now meet this doctrine of vicarious payment fairly,— consider it as if you heard it for the first time. If you will not be afraid of polarized words and ideas, you will see that *this* must be the result to most men of even the advanced doctrine, that God is an embodiment of justice or bargain, demanding strict payment, but willing to accept any gold, if it be gold. It breaks up the inner fastnesses of the man's soul, by pushing his ultimate responsibility upon another. It makes God fearful, not because I owe him, but because he will be sure to make his claim good somewhere. It makes a man false in the precise measure of his own essential meanness. So that it was perfectly natural for that wretched man in Philadelphia to plot all the week how to cheat his bank out of unlimited thousands, and then on the Sunday go to Girard College and snuffle to the boys, " Now, my young friends, I have come here to-day to try if I can save one soul;" because saving a soul and standing square in absolute personal righteousness is by such doctrine not essentially the same thing. In a word, it uncentres a man. It lowers lofty standards so that you need not climb up painfully to reach them; but just slide along on the dead level, and you are there. It fills the world with churches, but the Church with worldliness. The result is,—

> "God and the world we worship both together;
> Draw not our laws to him, but his to ours:
> Untrue to both, so prosperous in neither,
> A chilling summer bringing barren flowers."

So then we must —

> "Unwise in our distracted interests be;
> Strangers to God and true humanity."
> Too good for great things, and too great for good,
> Letting I dare not wait upon I would."

IV. But a far higher fear of God is to fear him as we fear the surgeon, who *must* cut out some dreadful gangrene in order to save the life. Such a fear as this really touches the outskirts of love, — it is love and fear blended. When I went to Fort Donelson to nurse our wounded men, it was my good fortune to be the personal attendant of a gentleman whose skill as a surgeon was only equalled by the wonderfully deep, loving tenderness of his heart, as it thrilled in every tone of his voice and every touch of his hand.* And it all comes up before me now, how

---

* My position as nurse for this gentleman, Dr. R. L. Rea, of this city, gave me such insight as inspired this poor tribute to his worth

he would come to the men, fearfully mangled as they were, and how the nerve would shrink and creep; and how, with a wise, hard, steady skill, he would cut to save life, forcing back tears of pity only that he might keep his eye clear for the delicate duty, speaking low words of cheer in tones heavy with tenderness; then, when all was over, and the poor fellows, fainting with pain knew that all was done that could be done, and done only with a severity whose touch was love, how they would look after the man as he went away, sending unspoken benedictions to attend him. Now, a fear like this is almost the loftiest fear of God that has come to the human soul. Here we find ourselves among all sorts of depravities. Sins that are as certainly shattering even to the body as the splint of a shell or a rifle-bullet, hit thousands of our fellows on every side. *They hit us.* We can all count some friend or kinsman who has been killed by sin as surely as if he had been shot down; and it may be not one of us can look back from the standpoint of forty

---

and goodness. He was one of a noble band, all full of the same spirit. I am glad to say such words of them, and all the more that I am sure they never expected to hear them.

years, and say, " I am willing to take the unalterable and eternal consequence of all my deeds done to man and woman, ever since I was a man." And this consciousness of something wrong in us, this sight of something wrong about us, makes havoc of the peace of the soul; we feel in our own life a thread of the common cancer.

Again, not sin only, but death, is fearful to many of us; we shrink from the touch of God, as the man shrinks from the surgeon's knife. It *is* doubtless some pain to enter into *any* life, and that is why we shrink from it. It must be some pain to the worm in the water to strip away the dear old shell in which it has lived for seventy years (the seventy years of a worm), to pierce out into the air and spread its wings, though the next moment it shall exult and sing as it floats in the wonderful new world, with the rich color, and the sunshine, and the unbounded gladness. Now there is this intuition of our intimate dependence on God in every soul. Are we in sin? God must help us out of it finally, in some quick, painful way, as the surgeon helps the sufferer. Our suffering appeals at once to his pity, his mercy, and his love. Are we in life? Through him we must brave the great change of our being, and begin to live again in some wonderful new way. So comes this fear of God, — at once a shrinking and a clinging, inevitable and fearful. And this is about as far as most liberal Christians go: they accept this life as a mystery of trouble, and expect that God, who has certainly brought them into it, will certainly help them through it. So, with a touch of terror, as a woman would trust herself in a frail boat on our lake because she believed in the captain, though the waters were turbulent and the sky dark, we trust ourselves to God, and bear the peril as bravely as we can, — not always quite sure that we shall win through, yet as the life deepens, watching, with ever-fresh trust, the pilot at the helm, sure, as the days wear on, that the master knows best what to do, and that we have only to bear the burden, meet the inevitable lot, and trust to the end.

V. Then, finally, there is a fear of God which is more of love than fear, — a fear that has *no* torment. There is an inspiration by which our duties rise up before us, vested in a nobleness like that which touches the landscape for a great painter.

The true artist works ever with a touch of fear. He stands at his task, his heart trembling with the great pulses of his conception. Carefully, fearfully, as if his soul were to be saved by it (as indeed in some measure it will be), he tries to bring out the mystery of truth and beauty. There is a deep gladness and a deep fear as, line by line, touching and retouching with infinite care, he perfects at last to the visible sight the vision of beauty that was in him. And he is fearful exactly as he sees the perfection of the thing he is trying to embody. A dauber has far less fear than Church when he paints Niagara. Now, believe me, God hides some ideal in every human soul. At some time in our life we feel a trembling, fearful longing to do some good thing. Life finds its noblest spring of excellence in this hidden impulse to do our best. There is a time when we are not content to be such merchants or doctors or lawyers as we see on the dead level or below it. The woman longs to glorify her womanhood as sister, wife, or mother. I say, in the heart of us all, there is this higher thought of life struggling for a realization. All at some time cry, "Not that I have already attained, or am already perfect," and *then* the fierce conflict of life begins. The tempter tells me that if I try to be an ideal merchant or lawyer or doctor I shall go under. If it is a rule to mix inferior wheat, and call it No. 1; to pull a rogue through in spite of justice, when all the world knows he is a rogue; to keep a patient lingering a little for an extra fee, — then I must do it, or I am not fit for this world. I must go where the wheat is all pure and plump, and the judge has a clean calendar, and the inhabitants never say, "I am sick." If the woman will not dress, and dance over ground enough to kill her if she had to walk it doing good, in order to secure some darling match for herself or daughter, then she must go where there is neither marrying nor giving in marriage. The young man must see life, or be a spoon. Friends, that is the devil, — the tempttation in the wilderness, that every soul must meet and faint and stagger under, in some form or other. But here, on the other side, is God, — God standing silently at the door all day long, — God whispering to the soul, that to be pure and true is to succeed in life, and whatever we get short of that will burn up like stubble, though the whole world try to save it. Now here is the fear of God that is loftiest of all. It comes to youth and maiden at the portals of life, to make them beautiful in all sweet sunny humanities, yet to keep them pure as the angels. It comes to the wedded man and wife whose little children are beginning to trouble the home, just as the angel troubled the waters in the ancient pool, that the home may be a fountain of healing for the hurts and bruises of the world; and it helps them to look into that future when those little pattering feet shall tramp strong and steady in the ranks of life, those voices breathe out comfort and inspiration for fainting souls, and those hands, now so restless with electric mischief, grow skilful in the achievements of the age. It whispers how it will lead you and help you, if you will but keep your soul open to it; how you shall be able to bring those children into the great ranks of God's holiest and best, as you take heed to that monitor. It comes to the aged, and brings sounds from over that golden sea beyond which abides their home. It tells them to listen to no tempter that would make the grave the end of all, but to keep an open, tremulous ear for the whispers that ever come from the upper world, when the turmoil of life is over and the pilgrim rests for a season. O friends, it is to every man and woman the still small voice, whispering whatever at that moment we *must* hear if we will live! Not shouting, but *whispering*, so that we must listen with a loving fear lest we miss the accent; not repeating louder for our heedlessness, but whispering, so that we must fear lest we miss the word. God with us, not as an Eastern despot, or a stern bargainer, or a painful helper, but a pleading love. Not the thunder, beating in terrific reverberations down the peaks of Sinai, but that gentle voice on the mount of the beatitudes, crying, "Blessed are the poor, blessed are the meek, blessed are the merciful, blessed are the mourners, blessed are the pure in heart, for they shall see God."

XI.

A TALK TO MOTHERS.

1 SAM. ii. 18, 19: "Samuel ministered before the Lord, being a child. Moreover, his mother made him a little coat, and brought it to him from year to year."

THIS is part of a most touching story, how God gave to a Hebrew mother a man-child, many years after her wedding; and the gift was such a gladness, that she dedicated him back to God, and carried him back to the temple, there to minister all his life. And once every year she made him a little coat, and carried it up to the temple herself, when she went to see her child, whom she called Samuel, which, being interpreted, is, "He who was asked of God."

We have three separate statements of the nature of a little child. The first is, that, in some way, it is utterly depraved and lost; not capable of conceiving one good thought, saying one good word, or doing one good thing, being —

"Sprung from the man whose guilty fall
Corrupts his race and taints us all."

This statement, to my mind, is untrue, for two reasons. The first is, that it clashes with the loftiest revelation ever made to our race about the child-nature. Jesus said, "Suffer the little children to come unto me, and forbid them not: for of such *is* the kingdom of heaven." One cannot help seeing here the inevitable logic. If the child is utterly depraved, and of such *is* the kingdom of heaven, wherein does the kingdom of heaven differ from the kingdom of hell?

I sat at my desk, trying to put my second and most impregnable objection, as it springs out of the nature of the little child itself, into words. And one sat at my feet, rich in the possession of a new toy; while another went and came, singing through the fresh spring morning. Then I said in my heart, "O God, my Father! when I can say that this morning sunshine, pouring into my room fresh from the fountains of thy light, is a horror of great darkness, and the voices of the singing birds are intended to echo to us the cry of lost souls; and that the ever-changing glory of spring, summer, autumn, and winter is but the ever-shifting shadow of the frown of God on a sin-stricken world, — then I can say that the light that comes out of the eyes of that little child, who has not yet framed its tongue to call me father, is the bale-fire of a soul already akin to the lost; and the sweet confidences of the other, the unlearned blasphemies of despair."

The second theory is one that I have heard from some liberal Christians, — that the heart and nature of a little child are like a fresh garden-mould in the spring-time. Nothing has sprung out of it: but the seeds of vice are already bedded down into it; and we must plant good seeds, and nurse them until there is a strong growth of the better promise, — carefully, all the while, weeding out whatever is bad as it comes to the surface. At the first glance, this seems to be about the truth. Still, I fear it has not come so much out of that true philosophy which is founded on a close observation of our nature, as it has come out of a desire not to differ so very far from those who denounce us heartily as unchristian.

Such an idea of the child-nature is, after all, a moderate theory of infant depravity; and as such I reject it, so far as it gives *any* preoccupation and predominance to sin, and accept the third theory, as the true and pure gospel about the child-nature; namely, that the kingdom of heaven, in a child, is like unto a man that sowed *good* seed in his field; but afterward, while men slept, his enemy came and sowed tares among the wheat, and went away; and when the blade sprung up, and brought forth fruit, then appeared the tares also. That is the true statement of this fact, my friends, as I understand it. The good seed is sown *first*, — good principles and powers are the first to be set down in the fresh, young heart; while even the tares themselves are not utterly worthless weeds, but degenerate wheat, a poorer grain, but never utterly useless or worthless; for the better kinds of it can be made into a rather bitter bread, while even the worst can be burnt up, and be made to enrich the ground for another harvest of the nobler grain. The good is primary, and purely good; the bad is secondary, and not totally bad. And every little child ministers before the Lord, and every mother makes his garments from year to year.

I propose to speak briefly on the nature and possibilities of this mother influence, what it is, and what it may be. And note, first of all, that while in after-life the father may come to an equal or even stronger influence over the child, — in the plastic morning of life, when the infant soul puts on its first robes of joy and love and faith and wonder, the hand of the mother alone is permitted to give them their rich quality and texture; and, to her loving and skilful eye only is left the decision of their comfort and adaptation to the ever-varying nature of every little one that comes into the world. God has made it so in his infinite and unfailing providence.

> "Women know
> The way to rear up children (to be just);
> They know a simple, merry, tender knack
> Of tying sashes, fitting baby-shoes,
> And stringing pretty words that make no sense,
> And kissing full sense into empty words;
> Which things are corals to cut life upon,
> Although such trifles. Children learn, by such,
> *Love's holy earnest* in a pretty play,
> And get not over-early solemnized.
> . . . .
> . . . . . . Fathers love as well,
> . . . . . but still with heavier brains,
> And wills more consciously responsible,
> And *not as wisely, since less foolishly.*"

To every little child, in the beginning, this

earth is without form and void; and the first great light that God brings out of the darkness is the face of its mother, and the first sound that ever enters the silent sea of the infant soul is the voice of the mother as she bends over it, endeavoring to find some answering glance and call of recognition. And God has made it so, that the first sure sound the mother ever hears breaking out of that silence, is more to her than the great harmonies that were heard when the morning stars sang together, and all the sons of God shouted for joy. So, how can we wonder that the tender nature of Christ gathered itself into grave rebuke to those who would hinder mothers from bringing little children to him, that he might put his hands upon them and bless them? To me, the question is not whether the children will or will not be benefited by that benediction, and so whether it is worth all that trouble and hindrance to the Master to let them come; but whether that most noble and tender of all souls shall acknowledge that most noble and tender of all things, — the longing of the mother for a blessing upon the child.

Here, then, is the great fact set clearly

before us. Mothers, your heart is the first Paradise to every little child God gives you; he finds rivers of water there, and the fruit and flowers of his earliest human world. While he can rest there, no wild beast can make him afraid; and when at last he eats of the inevitable knowledge of good and evil, and is fallen and naked and ashamed, your love may so clothe him, as he passes out of his Eden, that he will always live in hope of the Paradise regained. And so "we only never call him fatherless who has God and his mother."

Then, secondly, while it is eminently true, that the little child has such rich endowment, and you have such a wonderful pre-eminence, it is also true, that the possibilities open out two ways, — you may greatly blight his life, or you may greatly bless it. The garments that mothers fit on to the spirits of little children, like the garments that they fit to the outward form, only more certainly, have a great deal to do with that child's whole future life. Let me give you three instances out of many that are kept in the archives of the world.

What would you judge to be the foremost

thing in Washington? The obvious answer is, his perfect, spotless, radiant integrity. The man does not live in this world who believes that any letter or despatch or state paper will ever be found in any country, which, if well understood, can call this great quality into question, after he had come to the prime and power of his manhood, — as for that matter, at any time in his whole life. Now it is an instructive fact for mothers, that of the few books that have come down to us with which the mother of Washington surrounded her boy in early life, the one most worn and well used is a book on morals, by that eminent pattern of the old English integrity, Sir Matthew Hale; and the place where that book opens easiest, where it is most dog-eared and frail, is at a chapter on the great account which we must all give of the deeds done in the body. Before that boy went out of his home, his mother took care to stamp the image and superscription of integrity deeply on his soul.

What, after his great genius, would you mention as the most notable thing in William Ellery Channing? We answer at once, his constant loyalty to a broad, free, fearless examination of

every question that could present itself to him;
a frank confession of what he believed to be true
about it, no matter what was said against it; and
an active endeavor to make that truth a part of
his life. Channing testified, with a proud affection, of his mother: "She had the firmness to
examine the truth, to speak it, and to act upon
it, beyond all women I ever knew." And so it
was, that, when her frail boy must go out
into the battle, she had armed him with the
breastplate of righteousness and the helmet of
salvation.

What, again, after his genius, stands foremost
in the life of Byron? One answer only can be
given, — his utter want of faith in woman. That
one thing did more to turn his life into wormwood
and gall, than all beside. He lost faith, first of
all, in his mother. In and through his childhood,
it was his mother that clothed him in the poisoned
garments that so wofully penetrated through all
his after-life, and made him the most miserable
man in his generation.

And so one might go on reciting instances
almost endlessly, if it were needful, to show how
true it is, that the mother makes the man. What

then, positively, shall the mother do who will do her best?

I will answer this question first by noting what she shall *not* do. And I cannot say one thing before this, — that the spiritual garment she fashions for her little one from year to year shall not be *black*. All mothers know how long before their children can utter a word they can read gladness or gloom in the mother's face. Let her smile, and the child will laugh; let her look sad, and it will weep. Now, some mothers, if they have had great troubles or are much tried in their daily life, get into a habit of sadness that is like a second nature. The tone of their voice and the tenor of their talk is all in the pensive, minor key. They even "sigh when they thank God." They talk with unction of who is dead, and how young they were, and how many are sick, and what grief is abroad altogether on the earth. And the child listens to all that is said. The mother may think he does not care; but, if my own earliest memories are at all true to the common childhood, he *does care*. These things chill him through and through. I remember how I carried the terror of such a conversation in my heart once for days and days, long after the good woman who had spoken had forgotten all about it. Mothers, your children have no part or lot in that matter; death has no dominion over *them*, and will not have for this many a day to come: and it is foolish and wrong for you to lead them with you into its dark valley and shadow. If one of these little ones should be taken from you, it will be to him only as if he lay down to sleep. No sweet fruit of childhood can grow amid those grim shadows; he has his own little griefs, too, already: he does not need yours. So, as he stands before the Lord, and you fashion his spiritual garments from year to year, put plenty of gladness into them, — let the first fear wait for the first sin. In the kingdom of heaven, to which he now belongs, there is no death; his life is hid with Christ in God.

Then I would ask that the garment of spiritual influence, which you are ever fashioning, shall not be of the nature of a *straight-jacket*. Has your boy a heavy foot, a loud voice, a great appetite, a defiant way, and a burly presence altogether? Then thank God for it, more than if your husband had a farm where corn grows twelve feet high; your child has in him the making of a great and good man. The only fear is, that you will fail to meet the demand of this strong, grand nature, and try to break where you ought to build. The question for you to solve, mother, is not how to subdue him, but how to direct him. Sometimes mothers are really selfish: they refuse to pay the price for this noble growth of childhood. It is a sad mistake to suppose, that this sturdy daring must be bad; first the wheat, then the tares. Dr. Kane was a wonder of boisterous energy in childhood, climbing trees and roofs, projecting himself against all obstacles, until he got the name of being the worst boy in Branchtown; but time revealed the divinity of this rough life, when he bearded the ice-king in his own domain, and made himself a name in Arctic exploration second to none. The tumult, again, when Sydney Smith was a boy, was a marvel of boisterous clamor. But when that voice set itself to be heard in the "Edinburgh Review," it roused a whole kingdom; and the abundant vitality that set all distracted in childhood, so penetrated and informed the whole after-life, as to make its record one of the best biographies in the English tongue. Do not break your child's passionate temper, but direct it. God knows, by and by, he will need it all to batter down great wrongs, and plead and work for the great right. Do not fret and fear over the predominance of the animal above the spiritual nature: it is all right that it should be so at the start. The first man is of the earth, earthy; the second man is the Lord from heaven. First comes that which is natural, — or, as the better translation has it, first comes that which is animal; afterward, that which is spiritual. Do you know that the pure, the almost ethereal Channing was so full of this predominant animal nature in early childhood, that the first idea of glory in heaven, as he himself tells us, that ever dawned upon his mind, was in connection with an old colored cook. There is a good, wholesome oversight that is beautiful in all mothers; but the true root of that ought to be a great conviction, that our nature is loyal, and needs no breaking. We never break a young tree; and, thank God, deformity is the rare exception in the spirit, as in the form. Blessed is that mother who shall know this, and let every good gift of God in the little child have its own free play.

Then, positively, there is one most important principle that no mother can ever forget. A good and great man, whose children are remarkable for nobility and beauty, said to me once in a letter, "I count a great part of the grace in my children from a new reading of the old commandment. I read it always, 'Parents, obey your children in the Lord: for this is right.'" That I conceive to be especially the true reading for you, mothers. When he is altogether with you, his demands are especially sacred, and must be obeyed.

I shall not speak in any material sense; but, when the child begins to think, he at once begins to question. He is set here in a great universe of wonder and mystery, and he wants to know its meaning and the meaning of himself. But some mothers, when their children come to them with their questions in all good faith, either treat the question with levity, or get afraid, and reprove the little thing for asking. Mothers, this is all wrong. This is one of your rarest opportunities to clothe the spirit of your child in the fresh garments that will make him all beautiful, as he stands before the Lord. He can ask questions you cannot answer; but be sure that the questions that can be answered are best answered simply and directly. The soul hungers and thirsts to know: indeed, it must know. Those moments are the seed-time; and if you do not then cast in the wheat, the enemy will sow the tares.

Then, as this primitive woman would be evermore careful to meet the enlarged form of her child, as she went to see him stand before the Lord from year to year, will you be careful to meet the enlarged spirit of your child? I do fear for the mother who will not note how her child demands and needs ever new and larger confidences. The last thing mothers learn often is, that the child is always becoming less a child. It is a great blessing to that child whose mother can be well-timed, and yet perfectly delicate, in her revelations; who can know when to reveal truth and falsehood, nobility and meanness, purity and its opposite, — in thought and word, — yet not have the child look up in wonder to ask what she means; who can feel, in her prophetic and intuitive spirit, the true time for every thing, — that she is never too late, and never too soon; whose children will bless her, because her words were always more of a revelation than of a warning or a rebuke. Mothers, as I speak to you so of your great trust, I feel still more deeply your great reward; for you are greatly rewarded. As I have thought of what I should say to you of what you should be, I have seemed all the while only to be recalling what a mother once was to a child. For my spirit went back through many years to a little valley, "among the rocks and winding scaurs," where I saw a man and woman, in their early wedded prime, sitting together. And as I sat with them, watching their faces shine in the summer Sunday sunlight, they seemed to me as the faces of angels. Then the woman sang some words I have never forgotten, out of a sweet old Methodist hymn. These were the words:—

> "How happy is the pilgrim's lot!
> How free from every anxious thought,
> From worldly hope and fear!
> Confined to neither court nor cell,
> His soul disdains on earth to dwell;
> He only sojourns here."

And from that time, somehow, I knew, in a new way, that this was my mother. And now her hair is white as snow, and she bends, in the ripeness of her fruitful and graceful life, waiting for the angels to come and carry her, after her long widowhood, to another of the many mansions, where husband and sons are watching and waiting for her coming. And is not this what a million sons will tell of their mothers? Blessed is that man whose mother has made all mothers worshipful; blessed is that man who can make such an entry in his diary as this of Washington in his prime: "I got away, and spent the evening with my mother."

Mothers, you have great sorrows; but then you have an exceeding joy. To you, more than to fathers, belongs the responsibility; but to you, more than to them, comes the great reward. No cares, no tears, no efforts you make are ever really made in vain. When your child grows up to his manhood, if that is noble and beautiful, he will gladly say, "I owe it most of all to my mother." And, if it is lost and stricken with sin, he will fear above all the sorrow of his mother, or to meet his mother, or that she shall know of his sin. And the first pulses of his penitence will always come at the thought of his mother. And then if, after all your love and care, the silver cord is loosed, and the golden bowl broken, and your treasure is gathered into the safe keeping of the world to come, there may still come a solemn gladness, even through your woe, as you realize that he is not unclothed, but clothed upon. And you shall see the travail of your soul and be satisfied, because he is a nursling now of heaven.

> "For ever and for ever,
> All in a happy home;
> And there to stay a little while
> Till all the rest shall come.
> To lie within the light of God,
> Like a babe upon the breast,
> And the wicked cease from troubling,
> And the weary are at rest."

XII.

HEALING AND HURTING SHADOWS.

ACTS v. 15: "They brought the sick, and laid them that the shadow of Peter passing by might overshadow some of them."

THE incident chronicled in the text transpired in a time of strong excitement, when some fishermen of Galilee had sprung into what was as yet a very local prominence, and were melting and moulding men's hearts in the fire of a conversion fresh from heaven. They had done very great wonders under the pressure of that power for which we use the word "miracle," though it is about as indefinite as the Indian term, "big medicine." And these wonders were connected especially with the personal presence of one man, Peter. They roused the entire country-side. The sick and lame, it was rumored, had found a new life and health when this man touched them: then all who were sick, and all who had sick, began to hope. Vast numbers were instantly brought in to share the new blessing, far more than the mysterious power could cope with. There has almost always been a point at which the power to work these wonders becomes exhausted; but there is no boundary, thank God, for human hope and love. And so it was, that, for every one of these nameless sufferers, God had put sympathy and the longing to help them into some heart. Kindly hands ministered to them in the daytime: tireless watchers sat by them in the night. And these, seizing the great opportunity, came trooping in, bearing their sick with them, resolute to leave nothing untried that had a spark of hope in it. And, when there was no other hope that the blessing of healing would fall upon them, they brought their sick, and laid them where the *shadow* of Peter might touch them as he passed by.

And this, first of all, is a most touching thing, this solemn, silent trust in the shadow of a man. The curtain is lifted for a single instant. You see the fisherman pass in his homely garb. The sick are laid there in the narrow street, along which he is sure to come. You can observe the anxious attendants scanning the faces of the sufferers, to see if the tide of life rises ever so little.

A moment more, and the curtain falls: it is never lifted again. To us there is no result, — not a word that Peter's shadow did any good; that Peter said it was right or wrong for them to try so poor a chance; or that the experiment was ever tried again. And the incident has never been attached, like a steam-tug, to any dogma or doctrine, in order to drag it to the private wharf of a sectarian conclusion. The thing alone, just as it stands, is all that is left; and it is enough for my purpose, because it is the indication of a belief that stirred some human souls in old times, and ought to stir them still, — a belief that there is something in a shadow cast from one over another, of a deep and potent power; a deed done sometimes the hand has no part in; a word said the tongue never utters; a virtue going out of me, or a vice, apart from my determination; a shadow of my spirit and life, cast for good or evil, as certain and inseparable as my shadow on the wall.

And the bare fact, of itself, seems to be hinted, in many ways, to every man who will watch with care for what is going on under the surface of our life. For instance, there is some mysterious force by which men often move us in attraction or repulsion the first time we meet them, — cast a shadow of light or darkness we cannot account for, and cannot overcome. What these subtle influences are, no man has ever told us. We all learn to reverence such impressions, or rue it if we do not, because they are the shadow cast by a substance we cannot see, that is to act on us for bale or blessing. And —

> "I do not like thee, Doctor Fell;
> The reason why I cannot tell;
> But — I do not like thee, Doctor Fell," —

is the inner and instinctive verdict we pass on some men; probably, also, that some men pass on us. Their shadows hurt us: our shadows hurt them.

I have said, no man, so far, has been able to tell what this shadow is, or the substance out of which it springs. I presume it is as useless to search for it, as it is to search for the spring of the life itself. Perhaps it can never be made any clearer than by the oldest faith we can find concerning it, that it is the influence of the holy or the infernal spirit, as it is cast for good or evil out of the life of man.

But in this sense I do not propose to dwell on the question. I should love to speak to you about some healing and hurting shadows far more easily understood, — shadows of a mighty moment, this way or that, we are casting every day, know we are casting them, and ought to know what they are coming to be and to do, — shadows cast out of a perverted or a purified life and purpose; and so, in every way, of unspeakably vaster importance than the more occult, remote, and mysterious shadow these men and women in Jewry believed Peter cast, and we may believe we cast, in some fashion, while we may have no will at all in the thing we have done.

And, foremost of all shadows, of a greater bale or blessing than perhaps any other we can cast, is the shadow of the home; the place where father, mother, and children dwell together; where, four times in a century, God makes a new earth, and out of which he peoples a new heaven; the most holy place on earth, the place no wise man will ever enter with a profane or careless step.

I have sat bareheaded in the noblest Gothic cathedral on the earth, listening to a choir and organ that to me seemed as the voices of the singers, and the music that is heard, when the martyrs enter heaven. And for years I sat, in my youth, in a simple country church, on every Sunday morning, joining in the old liturgies, that, in one form or another, had been said and sung ever since the Saxon embraced the Christian faith. Just beside where I sat was a figure carven in stone, the memorial of a man who came home, five hundred and fifty years ago, all broken from fighting for the Holy Land in one of the Crusades, and was laid there in the tomb to wait for the resurrection. And out of the low, latticed windows I could look on a green graveyard, where the dust of Roman and Saxon, Dane and Englishman, rested, after life's fitful fever, within the shadow of the awful mystery. And once, I remember, I rose in the gray light, and stood alone by Niagara, while the sound of its mighty thunder rose up fresh and pure, unbroken as yet and undefiled by the clamor of those money-changers who deserve a whip of not very small cords for profaning that place, in which, of all places, the soul longs to be alone with her God And I feel no regret, that I did not realize how good the shadows are that were cast over me from those mighty waters, that noble temple, and that rustic church in which men and women have worshipped for a thousand years. I did feel those influences. These were sacred places. But the *most* sacred place, the holiest of all, the place whose shadow stretches over forty-five hundred miles of earth and sea, and forty years of time, and is still a shadow of healing, is a little place built of gray stone. It nestled under a hill that sheltered it from the blasts that came sweeping over the great moorlands out of the North. It was a cottage with one door, and two windows looking right into the eye of the South. A little clump of rose-bushes and a plum-tree grew fast by the door; and one branch of that tree, reaching up to the chamber-window, became, to a little child I used to know, what the tree of the knowledge of good and evil was to our first parents in Eden. For the branch once bore only one plum; and the good mother said, " My child, you must not eat that plum ; " and rather proud the man is yet, that the boy obeyed his mother, and never did eat the plum. And yet I am not sure that there is much room to be proud. It was as it is with some other fruits on that tree of knowledge. The little hands did not pluck the fruit; but the little nails pecked it, until it was not fit for anybody else to pluck. And so I am led to wonder sometimes, whether it was not the best thing after all for those first parents to plunge in as they did, and get done with their Paradise if they must, rather than "keep the word of promise to the ear, and break it to the sense." But there, in that bright little home, hung round with pictures of a marvellous execution, Moses with the tables, — which were crimson; and Peter with a long beard, — which was green. There, bending over the pictures in the great Bible, or listening to psalm or song or story, the child lived in the shadow of that home; and it became to him as the very gate of heaven, so dear and good, that no great cathedral, no grand scene in nature, no place for worship anywhere, can be what that gray-stone cottage was, when the world was young, when roses bloomed, and fruit ripened, and snow fell, as if it were by an understanding between the child and the Maker, — they were always so exactly what he wanted; and I doubt not there was such an understanding.

Friends, I wonder whether we have any deep consciousness of the shadows we are weaving about our children in the home; whether we ever ask ourselves, if, in the far future, when we are dead and gone, the shadow our home casts now will stretch over them for bane or blessing. It is possible we are full of anxiety to do our best, and to make our homes sacred to the children. We want them to come up right, to turn out good men and women, to be an honor and praise to the home out of which they sprang. But this is the pity and the danger, that, while we may not come short in any real duty of father and mother, we may yet cast no healing and sacramental shadow over the child. Believe me, friends, it was not in the words he said, in the pressure of the hand, in the kiss, that the blessing lay Jesus gave to the little ones, when he took them in his arms. So it is not in these, but in the shadow of my innermost, holiest self; in that which is to us what the perfume is to the flower, a soul within the soul,— it is that which, to the child, and in the home, is more than the tongue of men or angels, or prophecy or knowledge, or faith that will move mountains, or devotion that will give the body to be burned. I look back with wonder on that old time, and ask myself how it is that most of the things I suppose my father and mother built on especially to mould me to a right manhood are forgotten and lost out of my life. But the thing they hardly ever thought of, — the shadow of blessing cast by the home; the tender, unspoken love; the sacrifices made, and never thought of, it was so natural to make them; ten thousand little things, so simple as to attract no notice, and yet so sublime as I look back at them, — they fill my heart still and always with tenderness, when I remember them, and my eyes with tears. All these things, and all that belong to them, still come over me, and cast the shadow that forty years, many of them lived in a new world, cannot destroy.

I fear, few parents know what a supreme and holy thing is this shadow cast by the home, over, especially, the first seven years of this life of the child. I think the influence that comes in this way is the very breath and bread of life. I may do other things for duty or principle or religious training: they are all, by comparison, as when

I cut and trim and train a vine; and, when I let the sun shine and the rain fall on it, the one may aid the life; the other *is* the life. Steel and string are each good in their place; but what are they to sunshine? It is said, that a child, hearing once of heaven, and that his father would be there, replied, "Oh! then, I dinna want to gang." He did but express the holy instinct of a child, to whom the father may be all that is good, except just goodness, — be all any child can want, except what is indispensable, — that gracious atmosphere of blessing in the healing shadow it casts, without which even heaven would come to be intolerable.

But to make this question clear, if we can, let me open to you a glimpse of some shadows that are being cast in some homes every day, not over children alone, but over men and women also.

Here is a man who has been down town all day, in the full tide of care, that, from morning to night, floods the markets, offices, and streets of all our great cities. Tired, nervous, irritable, possibly a little disheartened, he starts for his home. If it is winter when he enters, there is a bit of bright fire, that makes a bad temper seem like a sin in the contrast; a noise of children, that is not dissonant; and an evident care for his comfort, telling, plainer than any words, how constantly he has been in the mind of the house-mother, while breasting the stress and strife of the day; while a low, sweet voice, that excellent thing in woman, greets him with words that ripple over the fevered spirit like cool water. And the man who can nurse a bad temper, after that, deserves to smart for it. There is no place on the earth, into which a man can go with such perfect assurance that he will feel the shadow of healing, as into such a home as that. It is the very gate of heaven.

But I will open another door. Here is a home into which the man goes with the same burden on him, heart-sick and weary in every nerve and fibre of his nature, to find no forethought, no comfort, no repose. When he enters the house, querulous questions meet him as to whether he has forgotten what he ought never to have been required to remember. Plaintive bewailings are made to him of the sad seventy-seventh disobedience of the children, or the radical depravity of the servants; and a whole platoon-fire of little things is shot at him, so sharp and ill-timed, that they touch the nerve like so many small needles. It is in such things as these that the shadows are cast, that hurt, but never heal; that drive thousands of men out of their homes into any place that will offer a prospect of comfort and peace, even for an hour.

But let me not be unfair. The evil shadow may just as certainly come from the man. Here is another man in the mood I have tried to touch, tired, irritable, probably savage. All day long, he has fretted at the bit; but society has held him in. He goes home too, but it is to spume out his temper. He carries his dark face into the parlor; and one glance at it, nay, the very sound of his foot, casts a shadow that can hurt, but can never heal. If his wife is silent, he calls her sulky: if she speaks, he snaps her. If his children come to him with innocent teasings he would give a year of his life some day to bring back again, they are pushed aside, or sent out of the room, or even — God forgive him — are smitten. He eats a moody dinner; takes a cigar, — bitter, I hope, and serves him right; takes a book, too, — not Charles Lamb or Charles

Dickens, I warrant you; and, in one evening, that man has cast a shadow he may pray, some day, in a great agony, may be removed, and not be heard.

But that this is not so everywhere, or generally, how many happy homes can gladly testify! Believe me, the shadows of healing are far more and better than the shadows that hurt. I am not here to cramp life and nature, and to tell you it is harder to cast a shadow of blessing than of bane. The nature of the shadow springs from the nature of the tree; and, in this world, the upas and the poison vine are only here and there, while the oak and the apple stand by every cottage-door. And so it is, that into the vast majority of homes, all over the earth, the husband and father comes, when the day is done, like the inpouring of a new life. He need only bring himself to be the most welcome guest. The wise men, who came only in the shadow of a star, did well to bring gold and frankincense and myrrh to insure their welcome, where the child lay; but the shepherds, who bore with them the shadow and song of the angels, needed no other gift.

Then, again, what shadows of healing fall, in their turn, from the children! It has been my lot to see a good deal of home-life. I have lived in the old world and the new, very intimately for thirty-five years, among the poor; and in these years, since I became your pastor, in your homes and others like them, all over this city and country, I have been able from this experience to draw only one conclusion. It is, that no affliction that can ever come through children ever equals that which comes with their utter absence; while the heaviest affliction to most, the death of the little one, often casts a shadow of healing that could come in no other way.

I went one day to see a poor German woman, whose children had all been down with scarlet fever. Four were getting well again; one was dead. And it was very touching to see how the shadow of that dead child had come over the mother, and sent its blessing of healing through all the springs of her life. "These are beautiful children," I said. — "Oh, yes! but 1 should have seen the one that died." — "Good?" — "Yes; but he was an angel. Patient had they been in their illness, — very patient; but I should have seen the lamb that was gone, — he was *so* patient." So, then, I saw how it was the shadow of healing had touched her from the babe in heaven. While he was with her, he was like the rest: she held them all alike in her heart, and overshadowed them all alike with her love. But now, when he was gone, he cast the shadow. The little shroud was turned into a white robe, that glistened and shone in the sun of Paradise, so that she was blinded; the broken prattle had filled out into an angel-song; the face shone as the face of an angel; and, all unknown to herself, God had laid her where the shadow of the little one up in heaven could touch her with its healing. And no shadow is so full of healing as that shadow of the child that is always a child in heaven. The most gentle and patient will sometimes feel a touch of irritation at the waywardness of the one that is with us; but no father or mother in this world ever did bring back any sense of such a feeling toward the one that is gone. The shadow of healing destroys it for ever. Nay, it may be, that, when some shadow that hurts has settled down, they can hardly tell how, between the father and mother, and holds hard on to the heart,—so that no prattle and laughter of the little ones in the home has power to lift and disperse it,—then one touch of that shadow cast from beyond the grave in one instant heals all the sickness.

> "As through the land at eve we went,
> And plucked the ripened ears,
> We fell out, my wife and I,—
> Oh, we fell out, I know not why,
> And kissed again with tears.
> For when we came where lies the babe
> We lost in former years,
> There, above the little grave,—
> There, above the little grave,—
> We kissed again with tears."

So it is in some way true, that my shadow, the shadow of my spirit and life, is a subtle and wonderful substance too. I think that in some deep, far-reaching way, if my word is true, but my heart false, the heart casts a shadow that robs the word of its finest essence, so that every true man I speak to finds it difficult to believe me. And if my word is gentle, but my heart is savage, the gentle word will not win on true hearts, because the shadow of what is not gentle will destroy its essence. But just as in the fine touch of nature, in one of the stories of Mr. Dickens, where a man is made to say the most savage and bitter things, while yet his heart is a wellspring of love and gentleness, and a small bird sits all the while on his shoulder, not in the least alarmed; so I may say hard things sometimes: if my heart is gentle, then the heart will cast the shadow, and will not even frighten a bird away.

Finally, within every healing shadow is God himself; and so, though it seem to be a shadow of the sorest sorrow and pain, as it was to that poor woman, yet will it lift *me* upward, and lead me into the light. Indeed it cannot be a hurting shadow, if God is in it. I care not how painful, perplexing, and dark, the very darkness will be light about me. If he is with me, I will fear no evil. All the shadows of God are divine.

> "Many shadows there be, but
>   Each points to the sun:
>   The shadows are many,
>   The sunlight is one.
>   Life's fortunes may fluctuate;
>   God's love does not;
>   And his love is unchanged,
>   While it changes our lot.
>   Let us look to the light
>   Which is common to all,
>   And down to the shadows
>   That ever do fall, —
>   Ay, even the darkest,
>   In this faith alone,
>   That in tracing the shadows,
>   We find out the sun."

I remember going once to our lake shore with my children, who had carried me off with them to play. And sitting down on a sand-bank, while they strayed along the margin of the waters, I gradually got into a waking dream about the mighty inland sea. I thought of the primitive era, when, by some new balancing of the internal fires, "God said, Let the waters be gathered together, and it was so; and God saw that it was good." But the picture I made of the scene was vast, dreary, and uncertain, as the waters of the lake seem to be on the edge of a wild winter night, with not a touch of beauty or blessing about it. Just then, the children came running to me with a treasure they had found in the sand. It was a small shell of exquisite beauty, bedded in a piece of limestone. It was a sermon in a stone. For it said to me, "I was born in the time you have just made so dreary. I was no more to that for which I was made than the garment is for your child. Yet you can see how beautiful I must have been, and then guess what blessing past your understanding was present in the world you have made so dark. Look at me, and repent of your incipient atheism, and believe that wherever there is life, let it be ever so mean and poor, there also is God. The whole round world, with all its life, is touched in some way by his shadow and his light."

XIII.

THE HITHER SIDE.

EXOD. xxxiii. 18, 20: "And Moses said, I beseech thee, show me thy glory. . . . And the Lord said, There shall no man see me, and live."

My text contains two things, — the desire of the man, and the answer of God. The desire of the man is for a full revelation of providence and grace from this side of his life, — from a starting-point: the answer of God is, that cannot be, because, if such a revelation was made, it would destroy the life itself.

Moses had been hidden away in the recesses of Midian, forty years, quietly feeding his flock and his family. He expected, doubtless, to die, as he had long lived, a shepherd. But the Divine Providence had marked out a very different path for him; and so he found himself compelled to come out of his rest, and head the great exodus of his kinsmen from Egypt. At the time when he uttered this prayer, a part of his work was done; but the hardest task was before him. The multitude was there; but it was a vast, uncouth mass of humanity, debased by the curse of slavery, under which it had long groaned; and depended on him almost as a babe depends on its mother, for the future. Moses feels what a deep responsibility rests upon him, — how fearfully he must fail if this movement is a failure, and what a glory will rest on his success if he succeeds. The solemn issue fills his heart with a great longing to know what it will be. So, with the simple trust of a man who believes that this issue is already as good as settled in the counsels of the Eternal, he cries, "I beseech thee, show me thy glory."

And I have taken the text, because it seems to 'me that this is always the longing of the responsible human soul, conscious that this life is welded into that which is to come. It is true that there are men who contrive to live on a semi-animal plane, who never feel this hunger to know the secret of the glory of life and God; but that is because the soul is dormant, curled in upon itself. And so, on the other hand, there are a few who have come to where this man stood forty years after, when he was on the mountain alone; the wilderness behind him, the land of promise before; and he rested at last with God, — men who sweep such mighty spaces in the spiritual heavens, and yet feel such a nearness to God on earth and in life, that they are satisfied: they have seen the Father, and it sufficeth them. But many of us, I trust, are not down so low as the lowest of those; and I know that most of us are not yet lifted into that great place with the highest. We are simply where this man was when he uttered his prayer, — at the hither side of what we are to do and to be. Life stretches out into the dim distance before us; and we feel that God is with us, though we cannot see him; that our life in the future is in his hand, while we cannot know what it will bring. We know that the cloud certainly has a silver lining; but the dark side is what turns most frequently toward us, and we long so much to see the silver. We say in our hearts, "If I could but grasp this idea of what I am and what I may be, my real relation to this life and to God, in all its fulness, — then, I think, there would be such an ever-present radiance with me, that I could never doubt, or grow weary.

My life would rise and swell into such full confidence as is only known to those that dwell where the Lord God is the light. I beseech thee, show me thy glory."

The young man in some way utters this cry as he enters upon his separate and responsible life, if he has any fair comprehension of what it is to be a man. In New England, you shall watch him, a child in his home,—a tiny fragment of mirth and mischief, no more conscious of or caring for the future than the bird that pours out its song in the old apple-tree fast by his chamber window. But the years sweep on in their wonderful, silent certainty. Childhood opens into youth. The school and college set their mark on his forehead, and he stands at last on the verge of his manhood, in that first prime, beautiful in the innocent as the first bloom on the grape. Watch him then: he can no more stay in the old home, than Noah could stay in the old ark, when he knew the earth was blossoming and waiting for him after the Flood. But, as he longs to go,—I speak from my own experience,—there are moments when this hunger for some revelation of what his life will be grows almost into a pain; when he feels, that one flash, clear through, would be worth a year of living. It is then that his soul wrestles with God, cries out to him, "I beseech thee, show me thy glory." Let me see whether I shall be like a tree planted by the rivers of water, or a mere stick left in the sand by the receding tide.

The young man and maiden stand with their hands clasped together, looking onward to that time, when the revelation they have made each to the other shall be made openly to the world, and they shall be, for ever after, man and wife. It is a wonder of happiness, as they stand there and look through the golden gates, down the long vista, from this first prime to that day when they shall be old and gray-headed, and gather up their feet and die. But then, after that, comes the longing to know what this life they are to live will be. It is with them as it was with the man Moses: the very sacredness of this life to come makes them anxious about its unfolding. "What if I should fail to be what I now seem to be? If poverty should come in at the door, and love fly out at the window? If one of us should die, or if in any way this fair morning should bring a noon of black cloud-banks and a night of storm and sorrow? In doubling my chances of blessedness, I am doubling my chances of wretchedness. The divine balances never kick the beam." It is when the man and woman feel so deeply this meaning that these questionings come; and, as they rise and press on the soul, they are this cry of the man to God, " I beseech thee, show me thy glory."

Life sweeps on again, and the father and mother bend over their first-born; that wonderful new testament from God out of heaven, the holiest and most beautiful thing to them this world ever held. They watch it as the lights and shadows ripple over the face, and the smile comes and goes that has so constantly suggested the nearer presence of the angels; and, as they watch, they wonder what will be the fruitage of this folded soul. Here is a life with them, and theirs that can never end.

> " The little lids now folded fast, —
> They must learn to drop at last
>   Our bitter, burning tears;
> That small, frail being, singly stand
>   At God's right hand,
> Lifting up those sleeping eyes,
> Dilated with great destinies."

They have the power, in their measure, to mould this life into the image of God, or to brand it with the mark of the beast; and the awfulness of their trust rises before them, as the future of Israel rose before Moses in the wilderness. Father, mother, child, they can never be separate. First it was one life, then two; now three mingle together, never again to be severed, father, mother, and child, now and for ever. No wonder that they long to know what will be the destiny of their trust, — the glory of God in this gift that he has sent them. If they could see that, they could live for ever content; and, with one heart and voice, they cry, "We beseech thee, show us thy glory."

There are those, again, who feel after this revelation upon their common life. There is a school of writers and thinkers, — at the head of which, in his lifetime, stood Mr. Thackeray, — who, getting on into middle life, are led to cry out mournfully, that life has lost its glow and glory; — has settled into a jog-trot joylessness; that their poetry sounds just like prose, and commonplace is written over the portals of every day.

Yet these men will never tire of telling you what life used to be when they were young, what it was to find the first bird's-nest and snow-drop in the spring, to go on summer picnics, to have the first sleigh-ride, to keep Thanksgiving in the old home, to receive certain letters, and to enter a certain parlor. Nay, in more tender moods, they can tell you what it was to kneel down before our Father, and have no more doubt of his listening, than they had of the mother's listening, on whose knees their hands were resting, of a time when they believed heaven was only a little ways out through the blue, and the sister, who had gone, looked and talked precisely as she had done on earth. But now they wear their rue with a difference. This bloom has gone, and they hold on for sheer duty. They find that their life has twisted itself into others past all unloosing. They cannot choose not to be what they are. "To be, or not to be," is not the question. They must *be*, and be steady and strong too, for the sake of others, if for nothing else. But what a difference would come to their living, if with that life in their youth, that was fresh every morning and re newed every evening, they could mingle this experience of their age, that seems to have driven it out! and that longing, when it comes, is this cry, " I beseech thee, show me thy glory."

Finally, in these days the patriot watches for a revelation of this glory on the nation. Inevitable, irresistible as the sweep of a planet, the mighty storm of war has smitten us, — routed us out of our old resting-places; and God has said to us, as he said to Moses, " Get thee out, thou and thy people." Surely this old Hebrew did not strive harder than we have done to stay where he was; not to go out at the bidding of the Lord; to be quiet, and let an infernal institution alone; to hold on to our mutton, and milk, and wool. But it is the everlasting alternative set before every great people, — the Red Sea and the wilderness, a baptism of fear and fire; then absolute obedience to God, and then at last victory, and the rest that remains, — or a peace purchased at a price that would make us a by-word and a hissing among the nations, and our future a blackness of darkness for ever. Thank God that we have known the day of our visitation, have found that we can only be in the line of providence through the Red Sea and the wilderness. But then the tremendous interests at stake touch us with this longing to know what is finally to come of it. The cry comes up to God from the nation, "I beseech thee, show me thy glory."

And so it is everywhere with the deeper heart: always we want to see the other from the hither side. Wherever a young man has left his home, to enter the battle of life; or a young man and maiden have said the most sacred word we ever say to each other; or a father and mother look into the face of their first-born; or a weary man holds on steady and true, not so much for himself, as for others; or the patriot looks wistfully at the great multitude heaving and struggling, with the thunder of Sinai above, the great desert before, and the promised land only in the far distance, — this to me is the interpretation of that cry out of the soul, "I beseech thee, show me thy glory."

Now to all this comes the answer of God: "This cannot be, for that would be death. Such a revelation as you are crying for, instead of being the inspiration, would be the destruction, of the life I have given you."

And I conceive a possible answer in the nature of the thing itself. Is it so universal, this mist on the track? Then it must be right. I might make sure of that, without any appeal, except to common human sense, and grace. The old pious conclusion, that what is universal must be best, is as good here as anywhere. It cannot be, that corn and trees are, as a rule, all right; and men and women, all wrong. If it were better that we should see clear through, from the hither to the other side, then to see would be the rule; and only not to see, the exception. No doctrine can be more divine, did we know it, than this of the fitness of things, — the essential harmony of the world and life with some vast purpose of the Maker. God is righteous (*right wise*) in all his ways. I do not envy either the philosophy or the faith, that can give evil such a dreadful advantage over good, as to concede to it any power beyond what pleases God. And no dilemma in the doctrine that this is the best possible world, can ever be so cruel as that which follows for ever, steady as its own shadow, the doctrine that it is the worst.

Then really, this is the way in which I act toward my own children. I never tell them all the secrets of my intention toward them, because a certain instinct I can never overpass tells me some reserve is better. If my son should come to me, as he started out in life, and say, " Father, I want to know the uttermost you mean to do for me under any circumstances; then, when I know how good you are, I shall not only be more content, but what I do will be done with more inspiration. I shall love you more, and serve you better, because you are so generous." I should count it a great misfortune to have the lad talk like that; and if I did so reveal all my purposes, and he should be ever so dutiful, I could never be sure that this was not dictated quite as much by the greed of what was to come, as by the love that springs out of our relation as father and son, — what I am now to him, and what he is to me ; and so the whole tenor of his life after that, in the shy springs and roots of it, would seem to be touched with the chill of death.

Then it is grander and holier not to know, yet to be high and pure all the same, walking by faith, and not by sight.

What makes the difference in our estimate of the first captain that ever sailed to these shores, and the man who brings his ship into port this morning? To the one, the reverence of all men will be given; but, to the other, hardly a second thought. The difference is this, of seeing and not seeing. The one starts on his dim and perilous way, breaking through league after league of trackless waters, and through the doubt and fear that is all about him in the ship. He has not received the promise, has not really seen it afar off; but it is no matter: the man holds fast to the hope set before him; and that keeps him steady, until at last his quest is found. But the captain who enters the harbor this morning knows what Columbus only believed. He has seen the end, as far as mortal can see that from the hither side. At noon or night, whenever he would look westward, here was the land standing in the sun; it was all plain sailing, well done by a common man, without any deep emotion, or struggle or victory, except over wind and storm.

But, once more, there is stronger reason in the fact, that what the man cries out for is

not so much something to *see*, as something to *be*;
and, until he is one with the glory, he cannot see
it. There is a wonderful suggestiveness in this
story, when you get at the heart of it. From
the time the cry is uttered, forty years come and
go, bringing ever new labor, and mostly sorrow.
Now he seems to be going backward, now forward; from the sea to the Jordan, from the Jordan to the sea. Working, watching, weeping,
praying, but never utterly broken down, he becomes at last an intimate part of the glory
he longed for. Then he does not ask for the
revelation he cannot choose, but have it because
he is in it.

Now, friend, does life go hard with you, and
this longing come painfully over you, consider
whether this may not also be your experience.
What moment is the highest in the life of the
Master? Is it when the angels come, or when
the voice is heard out of the cloud; or when
multitudes follow him, shouting " Hosanna ; " or
when great floods of life pour from him to refresh
the faint and sick and broken-hearted? Believe
me, not one of these, but that moment when, in
all the universe, he felt he was alone; that even

God had forsaken him; and yet was equal to the dreadful demand, and led captivity captive.

The solution of the problem turns on one thing only. As I stand here, looking wistfully onward, longing for the light, crying for the glory, am I able to step out in time with what is demanded of me as a man? When I have answered that question, I have answered all. God will see to the rest. There can be no fear but my life will pass into the ever-nearing glory; and, in the fulness of time, I am sure to receive the full revelation.

Here we are as the earth in the winter, and we cry out for the summer. Did you ever think how certainly the summer comes? The earth wheels onward through the awful spaces. We might imagine she would get adrift, or not set herself to the time, and so we might lose our summer. But steadily she turns to the sun when her time comes, and the glory breaks upon her, according to the promise. So at last she comes down from God, out of heaven, like a bride adorned for her wedding.

I get sick sometimes at my poor, halting faith, as I see how constantly God will remind me of the certainty of his presence; how even inanimate nature, as I call it, thrills and pulses with this ever present helpfulness, toward the glory that shall be revealed. As I did some little matter among my plants yesterday, I noticed, when one delicate shoot seemed to suffer from the sun, a leaf on the same stem came over, and covered it a little with its shadow. I tried to turn it back; but there was no shadow of turning. I could break it or fetter it, or inflict some other outrage on it; but I could not alter its will to succor that mite of a bud, and defend it from the sun; because it was as the wing of an angel, and its law and order as deep and sure as the law that holds the planets in their mighty harmony. Then, as I saw this, I said in my heart, "O my Father! let me learn from this leaf, if I will not be taught by thy Spirit, how the whole creation witnesses to the certainty of the coming glory. Surely if in this blind, dumb thing, there can be such faithfulness to the flowering; if this leaf can be as an angel, to guard and shelter the one purpose, — how much more shall I find, that the man, the most perfect flower of God, is guarded and guided, through the dark night and the fierce noon, to the full time when he shall unfold to the eternal beauty to which he was destined in his creation. For —

> "There's not a flower can grow upon the earth,
> Without a flower upon the spiritual side:
> All that we see is pattern of what shall be in the mount,
> Related royally, and built up to eterne significance.
>   There's nothing small:
> No lily, muffled hum of summer bee,
> But finds its coupling in the spinning stars;
> No pebble at your foot but proves a sphere;
> No chaffinch but implies a cherubim.
>   Earth is full of heaven,
> And every common bush a fire with God."

Young man, standing on the hither side, ready to start, and wondering what glory life will bring, believe me, it will bring all you can possibly use or deserve, in God's own good time. What is most essential as you stand there is, that you put heart and life into an honest and high endeavor. Trust in God as Moses did, let the way be ever so dark, and it shall come to pass that your life at last shall surpass even your longing; not, it may be, in the line of that longing, that shall be as it pleases God, but the glory is as sure as the grace; and the most ancient heavens are not more sure than that.

Man and woman, standing in the presence

of your first true love, do not fear any thing that love can bring. Passion might fly out of the window when poverty comes in at the door; but love will stand by you while life holds on, and then it will plume its wings, and go with you into the eternal life.

Father and mother, longing to know what your babe will be, it is most likely, if you did know, the very knowledge would interfere fatally with the divine intention. Only Mary seems to have *known* any thing about the glory, that like a star shone on the cradle of her son; and she could not understand it any more than the rest. You would be so appalled at the way he must go, the Sinai and the wilderness, the sorrow and pain; or so blinded by the glory that will come when he has taken his own place, — that, in either case, you would be totally unfit for the simple duties and cares, small and poor as they would then seem, on which every thing under God depends.

Man in middle life, to whom life is hard and dry, whose cry is sometimes, " O that I had wings like a dove! then would I flee away, and be at rest," — I doubt very seriously whether fleeing would do it. When Bierstadt wanted to get the glory of the Yo Semite into his canvas, he did not retire to his chamber and read about it, reclining on velvet and sipping nectar; but went out, over the plains, through the wilderness, through hardship and danger, into the heart of the glory; and watched and waited, day after day, if he might but see the skirts of the robe in which it was clad. And lo! he saw the glory; and it folded him in and was all about him, like the breath of life.

It is so that we must come to the sense of the deepness of the blessing of the life we live. Go into the heart of it, at whatever labor and pain; enter mightily into its duties; watch not for its shadow alone, as these complainers do, but most of all for its light, and it shall come to pass, that you shall find at last in your hearts what the painter found at last in his canvas, as much glory as will fill them full of a radiance that will bless wherever it shines.

Patriot, watching for the redemption of the nation from its fetters and sins, — I bid you remember, that, in this old history, one thing is exalted above all. It is not the power of David, the glory of Solomon, the reformation of Samuel or Nehemiah: it is this forty years' struggle through the wilderness, to which all look back in the after-time as the period when God came nearest, and his glory shone most gloriously; of which the very relics were kept most religiously, and the most awful days became national holidays. We may well thank God, and take courage, and march on, when we know that the pillars of cloud by day and of fire by night are set fast in the divine order, to guide us on the way. Perfect peace *will* come at last, and order and joy; and the glory has come through the thick darkness already when we rest in the promise of God. Let us all be sure, that all is well whatever comes, while we trust, and stand fast, and strive; and only hopeless, and rightly hopeless, when we want what we are in no wise willing to earn. The glory and glow of life come by right living; for in that "we all, beholding as in a glass the glory of the Lord, shall be changed into the same image, from glory to glory, as by the spirit of the Lord."

XIV.

THE BOOK OF PSALMS.

LUKE xx. 42: "The Book of Psalms."

THE Book of Psalms, and not the Psalms of David, is the most appropriate title. David is the author of a good many of the pieces; but he is only one of ten or perhaps twelve authors, who have a share in the entire collection. The particular process by which the book came to assume its present form has passed out of all memory and history. It is probable, that long ago there were at least five collections of Psalms, and that they were finally all brought together, and cast into one, very much as our collections of Hymns for the church service are made now. The Masorah, school of criticism among the Jews,— one object of which was to keep a jealous eye on the outward letter of their Bible, to count the books, words, and even letters of which it is composed, — has preserved the division lines of those minor books of Psalms. The same thing has been done in the Syriac Version, a very old translation from the Hebrew. It is also probable, that the editor had the trouble such men have now. St. Athanasius has preserved the tradition, that the present selection of one hundred and fifty was made out of three thousand Psalms, that were at that time getting themselves said and sung on the hills and in the valleys of old Jewry; from which we may infer, that bad verse and pretended inspiration is by no means the result of modern degeneracy. Who this devoted man was, is not at all certain: some say Hezekiah; some, Ezrah. Others say that it must have been an unknown man of a later time, as some of the Psalms bear marks of having been written as late as the age of the Maccabees, or about one hundred and fifty years before Christ, and two hundred and fifty after the last of the Prophets. The Jews themselves assert that the 92d Psalm was written by Adam; the 89th, by Abraham; the 110th by Melchizedek; the 90th and ten following, by Moses. Seventy-one are given to David, (some manuscripts give him eighty-two); the

72d and 127th, to Solomon; and the rest, to writers whose names you will not care to know.

This classification, however, will not bear criticism: the text itself, in some of the Psalms, makes it impossible. For instance, the Psalm attributed to Abraham makes frequent mention of David. Other and better systems, in later times, keep these elder men out of the book entirely, and make Moses the oldest writer whose poems are admitted. This is probably true, or as near as we shall ever be to the truth on this matter. Moses, David, Solomon, and seven obscurer men, answer to our call, when we say who are the authors of the Book of Psalms.

Then to come to the inner structure of the book, we may perceive that this editor has only been moderately careful in the performance of his task. There is, to be sure, a rough sort of harmony in which David has a section to himself. Then David has a share of a section with Asaph; then Asaph and others join at a third; and the fourth and fifth are by authors whose names are not known. But, by some strange oversight, the Psalms 14th and 53d are almost exactly alike: with the exception of a few words in one verse, they *are* the same Psalms. The last five verses of Psalm 40th are precisely the same as the five verses that compose Psalm 70th. Psalm 18th is the same as the 22d chapter of the second book of Samuel; while the 144th Psalm is made up out of a mosaic of verses, selected from the 8th, 18th, 39th, 102d, and some other Psalms,—the 8th and 11th verses of this Psalm being also the same verse repeated, and the whole composition standing without any perceptible harmony of verse to verse, or any relation of ideas each to the other.

Then, again, a number of the Psalms are written as you would write an acrostic: each verse begins with a particular letter of the Hebrew alphabet, from the first to the last. The long Psalm 119th is one of those, except that, in the the monkish division of the Bible, the alphabetic section is subdivided into eight verses. The 145th Psalm is another in which the acrostic form has been broken up by one verse being lost, — that is, the one set to the fifteenth letter,— but restored from some old manuscript since our common version got to be canonized. Finally, one or two other Psalms are the substantial repetition of the one thing, that any two versions of a poem from the French or German would be, when it was rendered into our own tongue. This is the outward frame-work of the book, as it stands, subjected to the honest eye-sight we give to any other book, — a selection of sacred poems, from a great mass, written during a range of years that would include the reign of Alfred the Great and the presidency of Abraham Lincoln, containing marks of carelessness that would ruin the reputation of any editor in our own time; with no particular certainty about the authorship, or when the book was collected, or who did it, or when men pronounced it of such divine authority, or who authorized them to do so, and whether some of the best among the two thousand eight hundred and fifty rejected Psalms ought not to have been retained, at any rate in preference to those that are twice printed.

Now, then, here is a most interesting study: all nations have grown into poetry as soon as they began to grow into any thing above the commonest life of the moment. But this book of poems has taken its place easily and beautifully before and over the home-poems of the foremost nations

on the globe. The Greek, by comparison, has
forgotten his Homer and Hesiod; the Roman,
those first poetic utterances out of which Livy
and those that followed him drew their material
for the beginnings of the history of that marvellous
commonwealth. The sagas of Scandinavia, and
the sacred hymns of the Druids, have all gone
into night. The psalms are lost that sounded
through the temple-services and palaces and cot-
tages of Egypt and Assyria. Even where the
sacred poem is left, the meaning is dead, or all
but dead, whether it be to the disciple of Buddha
or Mahomet; while here is a book of poems,
some of which are probably as old as the oldest
of those that are dying or dead, as fresh and wel-
come as ever. If I could have stood here this
morning, and, instead of my sermon, could have
told you that I had come into the possession of a
wonderful and curious literary treasure, that
had been sent to me, say from China, — a book
written from two to three thousand years ago, —
a book of poems by different authors, ranging
through a period of a thousand years, in which
there are to be found the most vivid pictures of
life in that old time; the writers, with the sim-

plicity of children, letting you look into their hearts, so that by looking, you learn their innermost experiences of hope and fear, sorrow and joy, struggle, defeat, and victory, their thoughts of life and death in its almost infinite differences to different men: and all this not as a description of a life they *stand and look at*, but a life in which they themselves are at once actors and spokesmen, as much as if Tennyson had been in the charge of the Light Brigade, or the foremost actor in the French Revolution had written the Marseillaise. That ever since those poems were written, they had exerted the most wonderful power over the human heart, — great armies had stood bare-headed to sing some of them before great battles, and knelt down to repeat others after great victories, — some filling out the aspirations of the loftiest and the holiest minds with words as pure as their purest thought; others expressing the deepest penitence of the most degraded, — alike welcome to the greatest king and the poorest beggars, — if I could tell you this, there would be but one thought in this church. Not one of you but would say, "Above all books, I desire to see that, and to get at the heart of it."

And if I should say to you, " Tell me what, in your estimation, is the one word that will best express the quality which has made this book what it is to all those different men and times," you would answer, " That word is *inspiration:* the poems that can be what you describe are inspired, and so are fountains of inspiration for that reason." And then, if I should say to you, " How can you be sure of this ? We cannot tell certainly who wrote them ; we cannot tell when they were collected ; no man can put his finger upon the time or place when the book was first said to be inspired ; it is badly put together ; some poems come in twice, and others bear marks of the most mechanical verse-grinding." Your answer would be, " This is all no matter. We should love to know who were the authors ; but they would gather lustre from the poems, not the poems from them. It is no matter when they were collected ; the fact *that* they *were* collected, and staid so, is the most significant ; and, if two thousand and five hundred years ago, the most notable men in Jewry had written in letters of gold that they were inspired, and the tablet were still to be seen among the treasures of the Vatican, that were nothing to this seal that has been set to their inspiration by untold millions of the race." Here, then, is the first principle in the inspiration and worth of the Book of Psalms to you and me. Whatever value we may set upon it, there is that property in it which I have illustrated in my ideal book from China, — perennial life and universal adaptation. Here are the very words that have sounded over the wild tumult of the battle, and dropped lovingly from the heart of the mother bending over her first-born, hushing it to rest, that are still unexhausted before the mightiest power of organ and choir, and yet have easily folded themselves to the measure of a broken voice on a death-bed, — a blessing of inspired utterance which Bacon and Milton and Cowper and Burns loved to set to the measures of our sweet English tongue, and at which no sincere heart ever came to drink, and went away weary and unrefreshed; because they came right out of the human soul, and go straight and fast as light, and high as God.

I do not forget, of course, in this discussion, that there are in this book the vindictive Psalms that have so sorely puzzled those that want to

measure the Bible's inspiration by mechanical
rule, and stand appalled, therefore, before the
terrible fury of that sentence : "Happy shall he
be that taketh thy little ones, and dasheth them
against the stones"; or this, — "As for those
that compass me about, let burning coals fall
upon them; let them be cast into the fire, into
deep pits, from which they cannot rise;" or this,
"My enemy has rewarded me evil for good, and
given me hatred for my love; therefore let his
prayer become sin; let his children be fatherless
and beggars and vagabonds for ever; let there be
none that will have mercy upon him, or upon his
fatherless children; let the iniquity of his fathers
be remembered; let not the sin of his mother be
blotted out." Now, there are some that say,
"These Psalms are a great mystery." And they
try to explain them by saying, "The writer was
a good man : therefore he could not, at the moment when he wrote these sentences, be personally under the influence of those feelings; else he
could not, on the other hand, be inspired of God.
We judge, therefore, that he uttered these words
as a prophetic foresight of what these men *would*
come to, and not what he wished they *might* come

to." I have searched through all sorts of books to find what this class of minds have to offer in explanation of these awful curses; and this is the best that I can find, — the best, I believe, that has ever been written. The reply to the whole matter is very short. We say, friends, you have a right to your own opinions; but, on the face of these Psalms, there is but one meaning to plain men; and that is, that they are stout, solid, compact cursing; a man cursing a man, — and that is the truth. You have every right to try to explain them away; but it is like biting a file, at once useless, and destructive of a precious gift of God. Your trouble rises out of your claim of entire inspiration of the divine, holy spirit through the whole book. We have no such trouble, because we make no such claim. We claim the holy spirit inspired what is holy and pure and tender and true, beautiful and good, and manly and womanly: but if there is a part of the book hard, unmerciful, vindictive, or ungodly, on the plain, wholesome interpretation of those terms as we live by them, then the holy spirit did not inspire that, but the unholy spirit; and, if you want scripture, I repeat for you those words of the

disciple, " Beloved, believe not every spirit; but
try the spirits whether they be of God." It is a
most painful instance of the sad result of consent-
ing to be fettered by the hard rules of a system,
in the interpretation of that book which, of
all others, asks for a clear eye and a free soul,
that the man who would laugh in your face
if you told him that the same spirit inspired
Burns to write his " Cotter's Saturday Night,"
and another poem which I must not even men-
tion, dare not question whether the same spirit
inspired the 109th Psalm and the 12th chap-
ter of Paul's Epistle to the Romans. To be
frank, however, it is but right to say, that there
are conceivable conditions in life, when these
imprecations become natural: when the poor hu-
manity, hunted and driven into a very insanity
of desperation, will take to this as the last effort
at self-defence or vengeance. I could think of
that slave-woman, in the old bad time, who mur-
dered her children to prevent them from being
carried back to their doom, using exactly such
words; but what is the true inspiration of such
fearful moments, has been set in a fastness of
light for all to see. When one had been be-

trayed, condemned in the face of all justice, scourged, blinded, mocked, smitten, spit upon, and crucified, he cried, "Father, forgive them: they know not what they do."

But, again, I say it is not for the faults or deformities of this book, but for its intrinsic beauty and truth, that the human heart is faithful to it, and loves it with such an enduring love. One great strain runs through almost every poem; namely, that this material universe, and this world and life, is not the mere cunning performance of a great upholsterer, but the actual expression of God. Written before men knew much about material laws, it is steady to the grand idea that God himself is the Law; so that whatever of terror or sublimity or beauty could be seen in nature, whatever of light and darkness in life, was interlinked with the presence and power of the divine spirit. Then, what is more, and still another beauty in the book, is, these ideas had been on fire in that human soul out of which the Psalm sprang. They had made the man sing; and this is the result of his singing, set to a music that is all aflame with the beauty and salt of truth. Travellers tell us what a deep meaning these poems gather, when you come to stand in the very scenes where they were written. The great multitude, for instance, on some day of high worship, stand in the portico of the temple, and witness a thunder-storm come sweeping up from the Mediterranean. It strikes Lebanon, and the cedars bend and break in the tempest. It drives down the sides of Hermon, roars through the wilderness, and, at last, breaks over Jerusalem in great torrents of rain. Then the sun comes out again, and all is still. But out of that thunder-storm there has come a Psalm: the mantle of inspiration has fallen on one in the multitude, and the 29th Psalm pours from his heart, — not as men sing of the storm now; for to him God informs and fills the storm: "The voice of the Lord is on the sea; the God of glory thundereth; the voice of the Lord breaketh the cedars; the voice of the Lord divideth the fire; the Lord shaketh the wilderness; the Lord will give strength to his people, and bless them with peace." The man quivers with this sense of the presence of God, and the quiver is in the poem too. The poet-shepherd follows his flock, guides them, defends them, seeks out new pastures, takes them through the grim passes where the wild beast lurks,— the valley of the shadow of death; he never for a moment fails of his care over them; and so, at last, on some high day of the soul,— perhaps after he has had a hard time, defending and seeing to his charge,— he fills with a great sense of his own relation to God, of dependence upon one above *him*, as he is above the flock; and the one spark has lighted up the whole beauty of the analogy: " The Lord is *my* shepherd: *I* shall not want. He maketh *me* to lie down in green pastures: he leadeth *me* beside the still waters. Yea, though *I* walk through the valley of the shadow of death, I will fear no evil. I am defended: my Shepherd has a rod and a staff. Surely, goodness and mercy shall follow *me* all the days of *my* life." And I wish I had room to notice a number more of those word-paintings, where some piece of life is at once made to shine out from the old, dim past, and is filled with the presence of God. There is the grand picture of a storm at sea; the touching sketch of the captives sitting under the willows on the banks of the Euphrates; and the sad wail of the poet,— far from the temple and its services, envying even the sparrow and swallow building about the capitals, — for the rest which he could never find, until he should meet again with the old familiar faces, and mingle in the services, — a sort of lamentation that I observe, poets seldom fall into any more, and as seldom into the services out of which it sprung. And so it comes to pass, because these men possessed these two great gifts, — first, that intense sympathy and oneness with what they describe, which makes their description an immortal, spiritual photograph; and, second, that wonderful realization of the direct presence and agency of God, by which they are able to say "I and we," where even Milton can only say "he and they." The best of those Psalms have for ever been, and perhaps will for ever be, abreast of every new man that comes into the world. They are nature and divinity set to music, — to a perfect natural music, — the key of which we bring into the world when we come. They will only die out, and be forgotten, when man ceases to wrestle and stagger under his burden, or to exult and clap his hands in his great moments of victory.

We shall for ever gather new insight into the

laws of nature; but, if we are imbued with the spirit of the Psalms, we shall never cease to hear the voice of God in the clang of the sea booming among the rocks; to see him in the light of the morning when the sun riseth, — the fair morning without clouds, with the tender grass springing out of the earth by the clear shining after rain. We shall measure the courses of the stars, and discover their great secrets more and more clearly in the ever-growing ages; but no attainment will ever carry us above that grand utterance, "The heavens declare the glory of God, and the firmament showeth his handiwork. There is no speech or language where their voice is not heard. The sun rejoices as a strong man to run a race, and there is nothing hid from his power." And men will for ever say, "I laid me down, and slept; for the Lord sustained me." And they will never forget to cry, "In the time when I am old and gray-headed, O God! do not forsake me." And, "As the hart panteth after the water-brook, even so panteth my soul after God," and, while there is danger, they will cry, "Keep me as the apple of thine eye; hide me under the shadow of thy wing;" while there is deliverance, men will tell how God " bowed the heavens, and came down," and " redeemed the souls of his servants, so that none of them that trusted in him were desolate." And, while ever there is death, there will be men who will be sure to sing, " My heart is glad, for thou wilt not leave my soul in the grave, nor suffer thine holy one to see corruption : therefore I will rest in hope. Thou wilt show me the path of life. I shall be satisfied when I awake in thy likeness."

And so I think it will be for ever with this book, studded all over with living sentences set to the music of living souls. The vindictive Psalms will die out ; we shall put them aside. They were the outpouring of hearts made savage by oppression in a savage time. They are nothing to us, or we to them. We could do better without them to-day. We can afford to have two psalms exactly alike, as we could afford to have two copies of the song, " To Mary in Heaven," in the same book. None of these things can trouble us, when we come with a sweet, wholesome frankness to this great book, and enter into the spirit and power of its utterances, wherever they chord with the longings and aspirations of the soul.

XV.

THE BATTLE-FIELD OF FORT DONELSON.

NARRATIVE SERMON, DELIVERED MARCH 2, 1862.

I PROPOSE to speak to you this morning about the battle-field at Fort Donelson, — of those that are alive and well there, those that are wounded and sick, and those that are dead. I do this because the subject fills my heart and mind above all others at this time; because you have a right to expect your pastor to tell you what reason justified him in leaving your church vacant last Sunday, without asking your permission; because I know nothing can be of so much interest to you as the story of my week's experience; and, finally, because the thing itself teaches the real divinity and gospel of the time.

It was natural, when the news was flashed into our city, that the great battle, as fierce, for the number engaged in it, and as protracted as Waterloo, was turned into a transcendent victory;

and when bells were ringing, banners waving, men shaking hands everywhere, and breaking into a laughter that ended in tears, and into tears that ended in laughter, — that we should all remember that this victory had been won at a terrible price; and that those bells, so jubilant to us, would be remembered by many a wife as the knell that told her she was a widow, by Rachels weeping for their children, and by desolate Davids uttering the old bitter cry, " Would to God I had died for thee, my son, my son!"

And it was natural, too, that we should remember, that there, on that battle-field, must be vast numbers, friends and foes, alike suffering great agonies, which we could do some small thing to mitigate, if we could only get there with such medicines and surgery, refreshment and sympathy, as God had poured into the bosom of our great city, pressed down, shaken together, and running over.

Sydney Smith has said that there would be a great many more good Samaritans in the world than there are, if we could be good Samaritans without the oil and the two pence. He might have said that there *are* a great many who give the oil and the two pence as gladly and readily as their great parabolic prototype; and it was a fine illustration of the sort of life we live almost unconsciously in these distant centres of a new civilization, that a great meeting should gather itself together without effort, provide the oil and the two pence in a wonderful plenty, find a great company of surgeons and others ready to leave every sort of indispensable work that they could not possibly have left the day before, and see them away on the very first train that started in the direction of the battle-field after we got the news of the victory.

Let me here point out the striking fact in our human nature, that while we are constantly inventing excuses why we will not do this thing or that, and putting the yoke of oxen or the piece of land we have just bought, or the wife we have just married or are about to marry, in the way of all sorts of divine things, there comes some great sweeping sorrow or joy, with its consequent duty, once and again in our life, before which our excuse goes down like a wall of cards. We can resist the marriage-supper; but a city afire, a great victory that will tell on the fate of the nation for all time to come, our own child in a fever, or a man buried in a well just as we are going past, flames over all excuses to the soundhearted man or woman. God seems to deal with us at such moments as we deal with our children after a long perversity. He sets us down in some place with a touch we know it is impossible to resist; and seems to say to us, "Now, sir, stand just there, and do just so."

It seems a trifle to mention, and I would pass it over, if I thought that reading about it would give you the sense of it; but it was not so with me, and I suppose is not with the most of you. You go down Lake Street over a deep, solid ice, take your seat in the cars, race over great, dreary reaches of snow-clad " prairie " and ice-bound waters, to step at last from the car into deep, soft mud, at the end of this wonderful iron road, and not a vestige of ice or snow is to be seen. It was the first time in my life that I got a clear realization of parallels of latitude. Our great desire, of course, was to get to Fort Donelson and to our work in the shortest possible time; and I am sure you will not thank me for a full account of Cairo, historical and descriptive. I will merely say, when you want to solicit a quiet place of retirement in the summer, do not even go to look at Cairo. I assure you, it will not suit. It is notable here only for being the first point where we met with traces of the great conflict. The first I saw were three or four of those long boxes, that hold only and always the same treasure; these were shells nailed together by comrades in the camp, I suppose, to send some brave man home. As I went past one lying on the sidewalk in the dreary rain and mud, I read on a card the name of a gallant officer who had fallen in the fight; and, as I stood for a moment to look at it, the soldier who had attended it came up, together with the brother of the dead man, who had been sent for to meet the body. It seemed there was some doubt whether this might not be some other of the half-dozen who had been labelled at once; and the coffin must be opened before it was taken away.

I glanced at the face of the living brother as he stood and gazed at the face of the dead; but I must not desecrate that sight by a description. He was his brother beloved, and he was dead; but he had fallen in a great battle, where treason bit the dust, and he was faithful unto death. He must have died instantly; for the wound was in a mortal place, and there was not one line or furrow to tell of a long agony, but a look like a quiet child, which told how the old confidence of Hebrew David, "I shall be satisfied when I wake in Thy likeness," was verified in all the confusion of the battle. God's finger touched him, and he slept; and —

> "The great intelligences fair
> That range above our mortal state,
> In circle round the blessed gate,
> Received and gave him welcome there."

One incident I remember, as we were detained at Cairo, that gave me a sense of how curiously the laughter and the tears of our lives are blended. I had hardly gone a square from that touching sight, when I came across a group of men gathered round a soldier wounded in the head. Nothing would satisfy them but to see the hurt; and the man, with perfect good nature, removed the bandage. It was a bullet-wound, very near the centre of the forehead; and the man declared the ball had flattened, and fallen off. "But," said a simple man eagerly, " why didn't the ball go into your head?"—" Sir," said the soldier proudly, " my head's too hard : a ball can't get through it !"

A journey of one hundred and sixty miles up the Ohio and Cumberland Rivers brought us to Fort Donelson ; and we got there at sunset. I went at once into the camp, and found there dear friends who used to sit in these pews, and had stood fast through all the thickest battle. They gave us coffee, which they drank as if it were nectar, and we as if it were senna.

A body of men drew up to see us, and demanded the inevitable " few remarks : " and we told them through our tears how proud and thankful they had made us, and what great tides of gladness had risen for them in our city, and wherever the tidings of victory had run ; and how our hands gave but a feeble pressure, our voices but a feeble echo, of the mighty spirit that was everywhere reaching out to greet those that were safe, to comfort the suffering, and to sorrow for the dead.

The " own correspondents " of the newspapers describe Fort Donelson just as if a man should say that water is a fluid, or granite a solid. I have seen no printed description of it that will make a picture in the mind. I think there is a picture graven on some silent soul, that will get itself printed some time. But it took years to get a word-picture of Dunbar, and it may take as long to get one of Donelson. If you take a bow, and tighten the string until it is very much over bent, and lay it down on a table, with the string toward you, it will give a faint idea of the breastworks; the river being to them what the cord is to the bow. At the right-hand corner, where the bow and cord join, is the famous water-battery, commanding a straight reach in the river of about a mile, where the gunboats must come up; and at the other end of the cord, up the river, lies the town of Dover.

It was my good fortune to go over the entire ground with a number of our friends, and to wander here and there alone at rare moments beside. The day I spent there was like one of our sweetest May-days. As I stood in a bit of secluded woodland, in the still morning, the spring birds sang as sweetly, and flitted about as merrily, as if no tempest of fire and smoke and terror had ever driven them in mortal haste away. In one place where the battle had raged, I found a little bunch of sweet bergamot, that had just put out its brown-blue leaves, rejoicing in its first resurrection; and a bed of daffodils, ready to unfold their golden robes to the sun: and the green grass in sunny places was fair to see. But, where great woods had cast their shadows, the necessities of attack and defence had made one haggard and almost universal ruin, — trees cut down into all sorts of wild confusion, torn and splintered by cannon-ball, trampled by horses and men, and crushed under the heavy wheels of artillery. One sad wreck covered all.

Of course, it was not possible to cover all the ground, or to cut down all the trees. But here and there, where the defenders would sweep a pass, where our brave men must come, all was bared for the work of death; and, where the battle had raged, the wreck was fearful.

Our ever-busy Mother Nature had already brought down great rains to wash the crimson stains from her bosom; and it was only in some blanket cast under the bushes, or some loose garment taken from a wounded man, that these most fearful sights were to be seen. But all over the field were strewn the implements of death, with garments, harness, shot and shell, dead horses, and the resting-places of dead men. Almost a week had passed since the battle, and most of the dead were buried. We heard of twos and threes, and in one place of eleven, still lying where they fell; and, as we rode down a lonely pass, we came to one waiting to be laid in the dust, and stopped for a moment to note the sad sight. Pray, look out from my eyes at him as he lies where he fell. You see by his garb that he is one of the rebel army; and, by the peculiar marks of that class, that he is a city rough. There is little about him to soften the grim picture that rises up before you, as he rests in perfect stillness by that fallen tree; but there is a shawl, coarse and homely, that must have belonged to some woman; and —

> "His hands are folded on his breast:
> There is no other thing expressed,
> But long disquiet merged in rest."

Will you still let me guide you through that scene as it comes up before me? That long mound, with pieces of board here and there, is a grave; and sixty-one of our brave fellows rest in it, side by side. Those pieces of board are the gravestones, and the chisel is a black-lead pencil. The queer, straggling letters tell you that the common soldier has done this, to preserve, for a few days at least, the memory of one who used to go out with him on the dangerous picket-guard, and sit with him by the camp-fire, and whisper to him, as they lay side by side in the tent through the still winter night, the hope he had before him when the war was over, or the trust in this comrade if he fell. There you see one large board, and in a beautiful, flowing hand, " John Olver, Thirty-first Illinois : " and you wonder for a moment whether the man who has so tried to surpass the rest was nursed at the same breast with John Olver; or whether John was a comrade, hearty and trusty beyond all price.

And you will observe that the dead are buried in companies, every man in his own company, side by side ; that the prisoners are sent out after the battle to bury their own dead ; but that our own men will not permit them to bury a fellow-soldier of the Union, but every man in this sacred cause is held sacred even for the grave.

And thus, on the crest of a hill, is the place

where the dwellers in that little town have buried *their* dead since ever they came to live on the bank of the river. White marble and gray limestone and decayed wooden monuments tell who rests beneath. There stands a gray stone, cut with these home-made letters, that tell you how William N. Ross died on the twenty-sixth day of March, 1814, in the twenty-sixth year of his age; and right alongside are the graves, newly made, of men who died last week in a strife which no wild imagining of this native man ever conceived possible in that quiet spot. Here, in the midst of the cemetery, the rebel officers have pitched their tents; for the place is one where a commander can see easily the greater part of the camp. Here is a tent where some woman has lived, for she has left a sewing-machine and a small churn; and not far away, you see a hapless kitten shot dead; and everywhere things that make you shudder, and fill you with sadness, over the wreck and ruin of war.

Here you meet a man who has been in command, and stood fast; and, when you say some simple word of praise to him in the name of all who love their country, he blushes and stammers like a woman, and tells you he tried to do his best; and, when we get to Mound City, we shall find a man racked with pain, who will forget to suffer in telling how this brave man you have just spoken to not only stood by his own regiment in a fierce storm of shot, but, when he saw a regiment near his own giving back because their officers showed the white feather, rode up to the regiment, hurled a mighty curse at those who were giving back, stood fast by the men in the thickest fight, and saved them; and, says the sick man with tears in his eyes, "I would rather be a private under him, than a captain under any other man."

I notice one feature in this camp, that I never saw before: the men do not swear and use profane words as they used to do. There is a little touch of seriousness about them. They are cheerful and hearty; and, in a few days, they will mostly fall back into the old bad habit so painful to hear: but they have been too near to the tremendous verities of hell and heaven on that battle-field, to turn them into small change for every-day use just yet. They have taken the

Eternal Name for common purposes a thousand times; and we feel as if we could say with Paul, "The times of this ignorance God passed by." But on that fearful day, when judgment-fires were all aflame, a voice said, "Be still, and know that I am God;" and they are still under the shadow of that awful name.

Now, friends, I can give you these hints and incidents, and many more if it were needful; but you must still be left without a picture of the battle-field, and I must hasten to the work we want to do. The little town of Dover was full of sick and wounded; and they, first of all, commanded our attention. I have seen too much of the soldier's life to expect much comfort for him; but we found even less than I expected among those who were huddled together there. There was no adequate comfort of any kind: many were laid on the floor, most were entirely unprovided with a change of linen, and not one had any proper nourishment. What we carried with us was welcome beyond all price. The policy of our commanders was to remove all the wounded on steamboats to Paducah, Mound City, and other places on the rivers; and it was a part of my duty, with several other gentlemen acting as surgeons and nurses, to attend one hundred and fifty-eight wounded men from Fort Donelson to Mound City.

I may not judge harshly of what should be done in a time of war like this in the West: it is very easy to be unfair. I will simply tell you, that, had it not been for the things sent up by the Sanitary Commission in the way of linen, and things sent by our citizens in the way of nourishment, I see no possibility by which those wounded men could have been lifted out of their bloodstained woollen garments saturated with wet and mud; or could have had any food and drink, except corn-mush, hard bread, and the turbid water of the river.

That long cabin of the steamboat is packed with wounded men, laid on each side, side by side, so close that you can hardly put one foot between the men to give them a drink or to cool their fearful hurts. Most of us have been hurt badly at some time in our life, and remember what tender and constant care we needed and got. If you will substitute a rather careless and clumsy man for the mother or wife who waited on you, and divide his time and attention among perhaps forty patients, you will be able to conceive something of what had been the condition of these poor travellers but for the Chicago Committee.

Here is one who has lost an arm, and there one who has lost a leg. This old man of sixty has been struck by a grape-shot, and that boy of eighteen has been shot through the lung. Here a noble-looking man has lived through a fearful bullet-wound just over the eye; and that poor German, who could never talk English so as to be readily understood, has been hit in the mouth, and has lost all hope of talking, except by signs.

That man with a shattered foot talks in the old dialect I spoke when I was a child; and, when I answer him in his own tongue, the words touch him like a sovereign medicine.

The doctor comes to this young man, and says quietly, "I think, my boy, I shall have to take your arm off;" and he cries out in a great agony, "O dear doctor! do save my arm!" and the doctor tells him he will try a little longer; and, when he has gone, the poor fellow says to me, "What *shall* I do if I lose my arm! I have a poor old mother at home, and there is no one to do any thing for her but me."

That man who has lost his arm is evidently sinking. As I lay wet linen on the poor stump, he tells me how " he has a wife and two children at home, and he has always tried to do right and to live a manly life." The good, simple heart is clearly trying to balance its accounts before it faces the great event which it feels to be not far distant. As I go past him, I see the face growing quieter; and at last good Mr. Williams, who has watched him to the end, tells me he put up his one hand, gently closed his own eyes, and then laid the hand across his breast, and died.

That boy in the corner, alone, suffers agony such as I may not tell. All day long, we hear his cries of pain through half the length of the boat; far into the night, the tide of anguish pours over him: but at last the pain is all gone; and he calls one of our number to him, and says, " I am going. I want you to please write a letter to my father: tell him I owe such a man two dollars and a half, and such a man owes me four dollars; and he must draw my pay, and keep it all for himself." Then he lay silently a little while, and, as the nurse wet his lips, said, " Oh, I should so like a drink out of my father's well!" and, in a moment, he had gone where angels gather immortality, —

" By Life's fair stream, fast by the throne of God."

And so all day long, with cooling water and soft linen, with morsels of food and sips of wine, with words of cheer and tender pity to every one, and most of all to those that were in the sorest need, we tried to do some small service for those that had done and suffered so much for us. Some are dead, and more will die; and some will live, and be strong men again: but I do not believe that one will forget our poor service in that terrible pain; while to us there came such a reward in the work as not one of us ever felt before, and we all felt that it was but a small fragment of the debt we owed to the brave men who had given life itself for our sacred cause.

Two or three things came out of this journey to the battle-field, that gave me some new thoughts and realizations. And first, in all honor, I realized more fully than you can do, that, in those victories of which Fort Donelson is the greatest, we have reached not only the turning-point, as we hope, of this dreadful war, but we have plucked the first-fruits of our Western civilization. I am not here to question for one moment the spirit and courage of our brothers in the East: the shade of Winthrop, noblest and knightliest man, the peer of Arthur for truth, of Richard for courage, and of Sidney for gentleness, would rise up to rebuke me. Ball's Bluff was worse than Balaklava as a criminal blunder, and equal to it in every quality of steady, hopeless courage. America will never breed a true man who will not weep as he reads the story of those hapless Harvard boys, whose clear eyes looked out at death steadily to the last, and who scorned to flinch. .

But here, on our own Western prairies and in our backwoods, we have been raising a new generation of men, whose name we never mentioned, under new influences, whose bearing we did not understand; and, the first time they could get a fair field and no favor, they sprang into the foremost soldiers in the land.

Good, elderly New-England ministers of our own faith have made it a point to speak, in Eastern conventions, of our hopeless struggle with the semi-savagery of these mighty wildernesses. My dear doctor, that boy of eighteen was born in the prairies, and went to meetings where you would have gone crazy with the noise of the mighty prayers and psalms; and he got the conversion which you do not believe in, and was a sort of Methodist or Baptist: but he stood like one of Napoleon's Old Guard through all the battle; and, when he was shot down and could fight no longer, his mighty spirit dragged the broken tabernacle into the bushes, and there he prayed with all his might, not for himself, but that the God of battles would give us the victory. That rough-looking man was wounded twice with ghastly hurts, and twice went from the surgeon back to the fight; and only gave up when the third shot crippled him beyond remedy.

"I saw those 'Iowa-Second' boys come on to charge the breastworks," said our friend Colonel Webster to us. "More than one regiment had been beaten back, and the fortunes of the day began to look very uncertain. They came on steadily, silently, through the storm of shot, closing up as their comrades fell: and without stopping to fire a single volley that might thin the ranks of the defenders, and make some gap by which they might pour into the fortress, they went down into the ditch, and clean over the defences; and there they stayed in spite of all."

One quiet-looking officer saw his company sorely thinned in the beginning of the day; and, that the cause might have one more arm, he took musket and ammunition from one who could use them no more, and fought at the head of his company, shot for shot, all day long: and, as a wounded soldier told me this through his pain, he added, " I tell you, sir, if that man ever runs for an office, I'll vote for him, sure."

Secondly, From all these experiences, I have got a fresh conviction of the great mystery of the shedding of blood for salvation. We have been accustomed, especially in Unitarian churches, to consider Paul's ideas about blood-shedding as the fruit of his education under a sacrificial Judaism; and that, again, as a twin-sister of barbarism: but as I went over this battle-field, and thought on the dead heroes and of all they died for, I kept repeating over each one, " He gave his life a ransom for many;" and I wondered, when I thought of how we had all gone astray as a people, and how inevitable this war had become in consequence, as the final test of the two great antagonisms, whether it may not be true in our national affairs as in a more universal sense, — "Without the shedding of blood, there is no remission of sins." And so, by consequence, every true hero fallen in this struggle for the right is also a saviour to the nation and the race.

Finally, I came to feel a more tender pity for the deluded men on the other side, and a more unutterable hatred of that vile thing that has made them what they are. On all sides I found young men, with faces as sweet and ingenuous as the faces of our own children, as open to sympathy, and, according to their light, as ready to give all they had for their cause.

I felt like weeping to see children of our noble mother so bare and poor and sad; to see their little villages, so different from those where the community is not tainted by the curse and proscription of human bondage; and I felt, more deeply than ever before, how for the sake of those men, who in spite of all are our brothers, this horrible curse and delusion of slavery ought to be routed utterly out of the land.

XVI.

OMEGA.

GEN. iii. 9: "Where art thou?"

THIS question was put first to the first man, as it has been, and will be, to all his descendants. It was put to Adam as he was closing one cycle of his life, and opening another. The innocence of ignorance had left him, and the insight which, for good or evil, always follows, had taken its place. The first man that ever did wrong, he was just then through his first wrong-doing; and it was with him as it has been with his children ever since: he was afraid to meet God with the sin on his soul.

This fact, in itself, would be food for the most pregnant meditation; but there is another matter, I think, still better at this particular time. The man is just completing one cycle of his life, I said, and entering another. It was inevitable it should be so, as the sunrise to-morrow. He tried to avoid it; but God would not let him avoid it. He never will. It would turn this earth into hell, if he did, right where we stand. "It is a fearful thing to fall into the hands of the living God:" it would be unspeakably more fearful not to fall into his hands, — to come to an end and a beginning with sin on the soul, and without the Holy Spirit to press that sin home painfully, and compel us to hide our faces for shame. I have heard preachers often try to make sin fearful by proclaiming a torture of fire for it; but the most fearful fire I ever heard of was one in which there was no torture; where a man had lain down on a lime-kiln, and the vapor had come up and destroyed all feeling, and then the fire; and, when morning came, what the fire had touched was charred bone, and the man never knew it, — never knew it, or he would have been saved.

And now, after these days of communion together, — some sad, and some joyful, but all, I trust, good, — we have come to an end and a beginning. When we meet again, it will be in another year. You have been busy, in these days, taking account of where you stand in your business. You will make very sure of that before you are through: it is right you should. "He that will not provide for his own household is worse than an infidel." Let all religious men remember, who let their affairs lie round loose, while others they count infidel keep things snug and true, that of the two, in Paul's estimation, the careless Christian is farthest from God. But those who are not careless in these matters, and will know just what they are worth, face to-day another question not less but more imperative, "What am I worth in the treasure of the inner life? how does that account stand? What I am worth *in* the world I shall make sure about; but then what I am worth *to* the world, and the world to me, demands still more close and careful investigation."

And I can well imagine, how, in helping you to answer this question, I might congratulate you, first of all, on the fact that you are another year nearer death and eternity. This must be the burden of all that is heard to-day from those who seem to believe it is the whole duty of man to show —

"How earth is foul, and heaven is gracious."

If they are right in their showing, there is a great outburst of congratulation through all Christendom, because one year more has gone, and presently the time will come when we shall exchange this life for another.

The lad, working at his tasks in the distant school, may love the school; but, on a tablet set in a corner of his heart, you will find written, "So many weeks since school began; only so many more, and then I go home." And the stout little heart beats faster, and the eyes grow misty, sometimes, with the happy anticipation. The pilgrim grows always more glad as he nears his Mecca or Jerusalem. The outer edge of the desert is seen with rapture by the traveller who has been jolting and rocking for days on the back of a grunting camel. The sailor, over half-way across the water, pledges the port he is bound for. There is no one thing I can think of, akin to our common comparisons between this world and another, that ought not to make us glad we are so much nearer done with this than ever we were before. Is this earth a desert land, — a valley and shadow of death, — an enemy's country? Is it true, as the Hymn-book has it, that —

> " Prickly thorns through all the ground
> And mortal poisons grow;
> And all the rivers, that are found,
> With dangerous waters flow"?

Then well may we be thankful, that we are so much nearer done with pains and poisons and dangers for ever and ever more.

And yet I doubt sincerely whether one sermon will be preached to-day, in which, from first to last, this doctrine will be pushed to its inevitable conclusion; whether one man will say, " Brethren, I congratulate you that soon you will die, and insist on your accepting my congratulations as the inevitable sequence of all I have said about earth and heaven since the first of January last." If the man would let his people alone, they might let the thing pass as one of the absurdities into which the best-regulated pulpits are liable to fall; but, if he insisted on a reply, it would probably be, " If that is the logic of your teaching this year, next year you must change your logic, or we will change our minister."

So this " Where art thou?" urges the preacher, first of all, to ascertain the worth of his own lessons. It comes to the pulpit before it comes to the pews; and, if in his own honest heart the preacher is aware that there is something wrong in this summing-up, he is bound to see where it is. He will see then that the result is wrong, because the statement is wrong. I dare not tell a man I am glad he is so much nearer his end, because I have been saying what is not true about his life. In the last test, God has seen to it, that nature should be stronger than such grace as that. I tell men this world is a valley of desolation,—a vain show; and its life a cross, a burden, and a disappointment: and that heaven is all that can be imagined and more of blessedness. Yet I dare not say then to my friend, "I am glad you are soon to die." What makes me afraid? Certainly, not that the future is not what I say, and infinitely more. The trouble is, I have got hold of a lopsided truth, when I make earth nought, and heaven every thing. And the truth is, this earth is my home now as certainly as heaven will be, and the life that now is a blessing as surely as that which is to come. This life is not a vapor, the flash of a shuttle through the loom, a tale that is told, a withered grass-blade; and the truest seer that ever looked into its heart,—Jesus Christ,—never said it was. It is the most solid

and certain thing I know of in this universe, after
the life of God. Is it a cross? it is also a crown.
Is it a burden? it is a blessing. Are there
thorns in it? there are roses. Do mortal poisons
grow in? let me find out their secret, and I can
make them divine medicines. The waters are
dangerous; but they make a province as the
garden of God, and power is given to breast them,
master them, and make them ministers. The
living swim: the dead only float. The leaf falls:
the young bud shoots. I am quoting Job sitting
in his ashes, when I say hard things about life;
not Jesus sitting on the Mount, or by the shore.
Let me be true in my living; then I shall rejoice
that I live, and shall not fear to die. A great
German has said, that "to the blessed eternity
itself there is no other handle than this instant."
Do I think of God as in heaven? he is here too,
or he is not there: of angels? angels are all
about me: of golden streets? I prefer green sward,
and so shall get it. Do I believe in heaven as
somewhere to go? it is first something to be.
Heaven is a temper, then a place. In a word, the
question, "Where art thou?" can find only one
answer from any fair-living man. I am in this

world, and am glad of it. The more I find it out, the more I believe in it, and thank God for it. And I mean to hold on to it as long as I can, just as a sound-hearted apple holds on to its tree, that I may get every ray of its sunlight, every moment of its darkness, every drop of its dew, and every dash of its wind and rain. The holy life is the life whole to this present world; keeping its laws, chording with its harmonies, true to it every time, and to the life that is in it; discerning always between the world and its wickedness, and holding on to the one with all my might, that I may be able to master the other, — as a good swimmer holds on to the water, and so destroys its power to hurt him.

On this ground I congratulate every earnest man and woman on the close of another year, not because it has lifted us out of life, but because it has lifted us into life, — not that we are older, but that we are more, — and not that the year has been all any one of us would wish it, either for ourselves, our friends, or our country; but that, in the great sweep of the eternal, it was the next thing to be and to do. So, in the light of a boundless life, of which this is but a small section, and in which a loving loyalty to this world, as God has made it, is a prime element for the blessedness of the life to come, I congratulate myself and you, that we have had another year of its influences, to abide with us for ever.

Then our question presents itself in another way. The fact that I am not to be hustled through my life, but to abide in it and love it, makes it imperative that I shall know how it is to be done. And I will say a word on that, first, in its most material aspects; after, as I may. When this fearful and wonderful frame was created, and became the visible sign of myself, there was hidden in its secret chambers so many years of life. I could begin from the day I became accountable, and use those years wisely; could write "value received" through my early manhood, my perfect prime, and my ripening age, at the foot of every one of them, and so use this world as not abusing it; or I could overdraw my account, as Burns did, and Byron, and many another, and close up before forty. This is what is commonly called fast living; and it is *fast* living: but if I have studied life to any purpose, that is by no means confined to the drunkard, debauchee, and black-leg. In the simple matter of using up two days in one, of exhausting the vital forces of life, of wasting more energy in one day than I can recover in one night, or in six days than I can recover in seven nights and a Sunday, — I can do that at the desk, the bar, the anvil, or the plough. And so, this day, if you are still young or in your prime, yet feel that you are not what you were in health and strength a year ago, my question, "Where art thou?" touches you. You are overdrawing your account, my friend; and, if you don't take care, you will be a bankrupt. There will come a day when you will find that nature has shut down on you, and will not listen to any plea of necessity. If you are predestined to live the mere life, but exhaust the vital life, you may drift on to seventy; but you have done at forty, and the rest will be only one weary drag; and no man can judge for you how much you can afford to spend. Every man must watch the balance for himself, and answer the question to God.

But let me not be misunderstood. There may come a time in the life of a man, when no consideration of how much life he is spending per day ought to weigh with him for a moment; any more than, in imperative need, he shall hesitate whether he will put himself in deadly peril, to defend some sacred trust; which his refusal to defend at any risk of life would render the rest of the life he might have to live worse than worthless.

But I am now speaking of that even responsibility that comes to us all,— of the every-day life; and the way a man may overdraw it, to make money, or win some bauble; or even to win some good prize in ten years, that ought to take him twenty. You say I do not mean to carry on in this way. I will turn over a new leaf; but I *must* have so much money first, or such a position, or have done such a thing. I have only one answer. You will probably get the money or the position: you may not; but the chances are you will. Then you will not turn over a new leaf; or, if you do, it may be too late. "Behold! now is the day of salvation." There never was a time when the temptation to be reckless of this life was so heavy and urgent as it is to-day; or when we needed so to hold on to the old steadfast idea, that a preacher shall be shut out, by the very tenure of his office, from the ordinary traffic of the world, that his eye may be clear, and his spirit unaffected by what dangerously affects those that wait on his ministry. It is a graver moral blunder for a pastor to speculate in corner lots or oil stocks, than if Gabriel came down from heaven to do it; because he stands nearer his people than Gabriel can hope to do; and the moment he casts himself into these great swirling currents of temptation, he loses the quality for which, above all things, they ought to value him, — the serene, unworldly heart. For it is impossible that even prayer can keep the preacher's spirit open, watchful, and tremulous to the ever-varying dangers of the times, if he is not in some way separate from them too; and he may be sure, that no exhortation he can give about a dangerous love of money can be more than sounding brass, when once he has touched the edge of the greed himself.

And be sure I do not say this that I may merely urge the husbanding of our powers, and the enjoyment of the fulness of our life, though that is a right good thing; but greatly because, by this means, we rise into the better life while we are still in this, and make a heaven about us of common blessing.

Scott wrote "Guy Mannering" in a few weeks. It is full of the aromatic sap of his genius. When he did this, he was in his perfect prime; his poems were but the forerunners of his best novels, and these novels are the crown of glory on his life. But Scott had one fatal greed: he wanted to create Abbotsford, as it were, in a day. There was no glory in this, as there is no glory in the million things a million other men have done, who might have done better. But, to make Abbotsford, he used up two days in one,— poured out book after book with a prodigality that astonished the world. The result was, that Scott, who had the frame and stamina of a giant, began to break down. In this there were two results: first, loss of health, that concerned Scott rather than the world; second, loss of inspiration, that concerned the world as much or even more than the man. For, just as the man lost his vitality, the new books lost their peculiar and perfect power. They deteriorated from genius to talent, and from talent to common place; and then the spell that had held the world, lifted men into better atmospheres, and quickened and nurtured human souls, was gone. Abbotsford was created, and then, after that, redeemed; but the world was the loser by all it had a right to expect of its noble son. If, instead of driving and draining his genius like a slave, he had waited reverently for its welling, then, when the sweet waters ran freely, had turned them into the golden channels of great books, for the blessing of the world, he ought to have written his last books as he wrote his first, — as he was moved by the Holy Ghost. He did write them as he was moved by his publishers. The consequence was, that the publishers got the book; but the world did not get that without which it was as worthless as a book of old sermons.

I mention this as an illustration of the deeper meaning of my question. In such a life as that of Channing, there seems to be an intimate relation between the frail and delicate organism and the transcendent genius. We are at a loss to guess whether such a soul could find a fitting instrument in any other body, — whether it could pierce and soar so, imprisoned in the mould of common men. But I conceive this to be universally true: if a man begins life with a powerful soul in a powerful frame, and then wastes that frame in a reckless disregard of those laws on which it depends, — then the failing human power to eat and drink and run and laugh and sleep and whistle and sing, is the indication of a failing spiritual power, of which these are but the signs. He is a full-orbed man no longer: what he has lost is but a shadow of what the world has lost in him. He may intensify as he becomes unwell, and run morbidly to some one thing, as a Strasburg goose runs to liver, — may become notable for that one thing for a time, among men as morbid as himself. But he has lost the most celestial thing, in trying to create the more material; as Scott lost the power to write books like "Old Mortality," in the morbid desire to create Abbotsford.

I do not, therefore, ask so much what is to be the result of any waste of power to you; that is your own business: but what will it be to your home and the world at large. Out of your life there flows, every day, some spiritual influ-

ence, as true in its nature and degree as any
ever known. You may never write a book or
even a letter; but then no more did Jesus Christ.
No mistake can be greater than to suppose, that
I have done my duty by my home, in filling it
with plenty; or my children, in securing for
them the best teachers; or that I have been
true to my marriage vow, because I have kept
myself pure, and never stinted my wife in her
expenses; or to Church and State, because I
have voted right on election day, and been, in
my time, a deacon. O friend! I tell you, un-
speakably more than this is that mysterious and
most holy influence of a sound, elastic, cheerful
human soul in a body to match. I see, once in
a while, a home in which I am just as sure it is
impossible for the children to go radically wrong,
as it is for the planet to turn the other way on
her axis. The whole law of their life, of their
spiritual gravitation, is fixed by the strong, sweet
father and mother; resolute, above all, to pre-
serve this perfect right attraction, though there
may be less, at last, in counted dollars.

I have seen men as full of chivalric and loving
attention to their wives, as tender and thought-

ful and delicate as in the old courting days, when their fate still hung on the woman's will. I see men sometimes in society, who will let no pressure of business or care crowd them so that they cannot afford time for sympathy, and to give a helping hand in matters that are above the price of money, giving what money cannot buy, — the light and life of an unworn nature. And all this is what I would ask most urgently in my question, Where art *thou?*

Is the tide of success in your profession flooding out your home, and human sympathies, and excellences? Have you less time for a thoughtful loving-kindness toward others than you once had? less time for your children, to chat with them, and play with them, and tell them stories? less time to give to your wife, who has, perhaps, been waiting all day, with a budget of things to tell you, — of no interest to you, probably, in the abstract, but the current coin of her little domestic world and life.

You may be too much done over to care for any of these things: then I will tell you what will happen. After a while, your children will cease to tease you, or your wife to tell you what is in her heart; and a cloud will settle on your home and its life you cannot account for; the old Eden look will leave it, thorns and thistles will spring up about it; every thing will change to your altered nature. And then, instead of looking right in the eyes of the trouble, and trying to amend it, you will do what this first man did in similar circumstances, — turn round and blame your wife.

Dear friend, whether man or woman, I ask you, as we part, whether you have kept this old wholesome faith in, and love for, the life that now is; because I really know of no way so sure to the loftiest and holiest life of heaven, as that which lies directly through a deep, quick sympathy with the life on earth. When we lose that, we lose what the sap is to the tree; the mediator between our being and the life about us and above us; the secret of all our growth and fruitfulness, as of all our glory and joy.

And I have said not a word to the hearers of my sermon I do not say to the readers of my book.

THE END.